Mother's Book of Home Economics

Books by Mrs. White

Mother's Faith

For the Love of Christian Homemaking

The Prentiss Study (Free Download)

Early Morning Revival Challenge

Mother's Book of Home Economics

[Cover photo: A wood stove in Mrs. White's Vermont home]

Mother's Book of Home Economics

Remembrances, Letters, and Essays
from a New England Housewife

The Legacy of Home Press
puritanlight@gmail.com

The content of this book is gathered from previously published posts from The Legacy of Home blog, written by Mrs. Sharon White. These were published online during the years of 2009 to 2013.

The Legacy of Home Press
ISBN-13: 978-0615889061
ISBN-10: 0615889069
Mother's Book of Home Economics
Author - Mrs. Sharon White

Contents

Mother's Book of Home Economics

Mother's Book of Home Economics

Mother's Book of Home Economics

Introduction

There are many Home Economics books that will teach you important facts, such as how to get out a stain; how to clean your oven; or how to read food labels. This is all valuable information. We should certainly have those kinds of books in our homes. Nonetheless, did you ever just want to enter someone's home and observe how it all works in daily life? Did you ever want to learn about how a family *used to* keep house, or how it is working today?

"Mother's Book of Home Economics" will give you that personal touch of Homemaking. It covers subjects like Marriage, Cleaning, Child Care, Manners, Simple Living, Motherhood, Thrift and Holiness. Here you will find a variety of letters, essays and memories about Home Economics. This was written by a New England Housewife, who has been married for more than 25 years.

Mrs. White wrote these chapters over a period of four years. They were mostly written early in the morning from her Vermont home. Each was published on her blog, "The Legacy of Home." They are now gathered here, in one place, where they will be easy to find.

There is an Index at the back of the book, loosely categorizing them by topic.

The writings are designed to encourage the Christian housewife. You will feel supported in your decision to stay home and care for your family. You will also notice a gentle nudging to live the old paths, and find peace there. Rather than following the modern culture, which is rampant with feminism.

1

Housekeeping Staff

Wealthy families would employ a butler, a maid and a cook. There might even be a gardener and a chauffeur. These homes were lovely places and were well-kept. It was pleasant to have company over and enjoy the surroundings of a nicely - run home.

Each employee had specific jobs:

The Butler -

He was sort of like the administration staff and the host, all in one. He would answer the door, handle phone calls, and sort the mail. He would get tea, or direct the staff in what the boss needed.

The Maid -

This quiet worker, did all the housework. She was in charge of laundry, washing floors, making beds, polishing furniture and keeping the house in lovely condition.

The Cook -

The cook had to plan the meals (based on the direction of the boss), get the shopping done, cook and bake, and serve the food. The cook was also responsible for keeping her domain clean and neat.

Mother's Book of Home Economics

The Gardener -

He would tend the flowers, mow the grounds, remove weeds, handle bushes, plants and trees. He was responsible for keeping the property in beautiful shape.

The Chauffeur -

The driver took family members wherever they needed to go. This freed the passengers from worrying about getting places. They could relax in the car, do paperwork, enjoy the view and just relax. (He also kept the car polished, clean and in excellent working order.)

Each worker served the family in a quiet, respectful way. They did not intrude on the family's privacy. The best workers did not gossip about their boss to the neighbors. They protected the privacy and dignity of the family. Most of all, they did not voice their opinions or complain about their work. They were greatly skilled and trained in their profession and were an asset to the home.

When times got tough, some of these families had to let the staff go. This left the family, itself, to take on all the jobs. Mothers, Fathers and children learned how to run their own homes. They were weary, but took on the tasks as a challenge and did their best to keep things looking proper and pleasant.

Over the years, families forgot about having a trained housekeeping staff. They started to slack on all the jobs until a "lived-in" (messy) house became the joke of American culture. It became the norm. People with lovely homes were ridiculed and made fun of for being "perfect" or "dull." Somewhere along the line, we forgot how beautiful it can be to have a well-kept home, which would make even the traditional housekeeping staff proud.

The next time you have to "*open your own door,*" or "*cook your own food,*" or "*drive yourself somewhere,*" please think of the domestic employees who do this for a living. Do each task as if it were your profession, and bring back the loveliness and pride of home.

2

The Cleanest House Ever

I have a wonderful idea to maintain a clean house. I came up with a fun way to keep the children busy and get the cleanest house ever!

Here's the plan:

1. I will come up with every single possible chore and make *chore cards*. Possibly hundreds!

2. One chore will be written on one index card. Here is an example: "Go through the house searching for cobwebs and destroy them!" .... or ... "Clean all the window sills.".... or... "Clean out the car" . . . or . . . "Organize the bookcase."

3. I will have 5 days of heavy cleaning. We will only do this on weekdays. I have an index card file box, and a days- of- the week divider tabs. - Monday through Friday.

4. I will put an equal amount of chore cards behind each day's file.

Now here is the fun part. I don't have to do any of the chores! These are for the children only.

This is how it will go:

On each weekday morning, after breakfast, I will pull out the index card file box. I will take out all of that day's chore cards. I will shuffle them and hold them up (like a deck of cards) with the words facing me, so the children cannot see them. I will let each child pick 3 or 4 cards for the day. They will have no idea what they are getting until they look at them. All the work will have to be finished before lunch. What fun! (Mom, make sure you are busy in that kitchen, making a wonderful, rewarding lunch for those dear, hard-working children!)

I can just imagine it . . . One child will be out in the car, polishing the dashboard, while someone else takes out the trash and vacuums the floors. Another will be washing all the windows in the house . . . A teenager will be sweeping down the stairs.

This is a dream come true!

What will make this fun for the children, you ask? Well, the excitement of never knowing what chore they will end up with!

You might want to include a couple of random chore cards that say things like, "Bake cookies and eat two of them before you tell us they are ready." ... Or .... "Make everyone an ice cream cone." ..... This will keep things exciting!

How about you? Are you ready to have the cleanest house ever?

3

Saturday Morning Chores

In my childhood home, we had a cleaning routine each Saturday morning. We would wake up to find a list on the kitchen table. Mother would be out on an errand so we used the list as our guide.

The first thing I did was dust our piano. It was in the large living room. There was an antique mirror on the wall right above that piano. I would clean the mirror, dust the piano and polish the stool. Right beside the piano was a beautiful china cabinet with the most lovely dishes on display. We never used them. They were part of our family heritage. I cleaned the glass windows on the doors, while dreaming about having a home of my own someday. I was in my own little world while I cleaned on those quiet mornings.

Next, I had to sweep down the stairs. We had an enclosed side porch, which faced the ocean. We lived on the harbor side of Boston, in a lovely small town - called Hingham. From the second floor of our house, as I worked on the porch, I could see ships going by. I loved to look at the ocean and enjoyed the sense of peace it gave me. I used to clean that porch for fun. We had all these lovely cabinets at the end of the room, near the stairs. This house was the same house my Mother grew up in. It had been a small summer cottage, but Grandpa had added on and made it larger. You could see all the touches and creations he added. I am sure the cabinets were built by

Mother's Book of Home Economics

him and they were darling. I used to clear the built-up clutter and tidy that area. Then I would sweep down the wooden stairs, all the way down to the first floor.

My next job was the bathroom. I had to scrub the entire tub. It never took long. It was good exercise. Dad had remodeled it at one point so we had sliding glass doors on the tub. I loved to clean that glass! It was a pretty bathroom.

Later, Mother would come home from her errand and start cleaning. She did laundry, cleaned the kitchen, vacuumed and made things look neat. It was nice for us all to work on our own tasks, in our own way.

Nothing in our home was elegant. It was a charming summer cottage that had been built up over time by Grandpa. It was a large house with 3 bedrooms upstairs, two porches, a large kitchen and living room and one bathroom. On the first floor, we had another bedroom, the utility room, a bathroom and a cozy apartment with it's own entry. We used the apartment like it was another bedroom. It was my brother's room for years, when he was a teenager. Then my sister took over. I was offered that room, but didn't want to be so far away from the rest of the family.

We had an acre of land, a garden and a large garage where Dad often worked. It was a wonderful home and I enjoyed daydreaming, while I cleaned on those Saturday mornings.

Mother's Book of Home Economics

4

Hand-Sewing and Relaxing at Home

I have a chair in my dining room where I keep my latest hand-sewing project. Right now I am working on a pretty pink apron. It has little white hearts all over it. It is to be my *cheerful* apron. I enjoy the process of slowly making delicate stitches. But it takes me several weeks to complete the project.

I am not as young as I used to be. Years ago, I could hand-sew an apron in just a couple of days. Not anymore. My hands get tired, they swell up, and I wear out easily.

But patience is a precious blessing. If I can sew a little bit each week, I feel relaxed and at peace while I am staying home. It is a delight to have a project where I can create something beautiful with my own hands.

This patience helps me submit to weightier matters. If am in the *habit* of being patient, I understand that things take time. I do not want to rush anything. Hurrying only causes stress. We cannot hurry decisions, or results. So in a sense, my hand-sewing project reinforces a serious character trait we all need.

While I am sewing, in my favorite chair near the hearth, a feeling of gratefulness overcomes me. I am thankful to be at home. I am quiet and content. I am *happy*.

5

The Bills in the Whitman's Box

Yesterday I ate the last chocolate. Holding the Whitman's Box made me almost nostalgic. I didn't want to throw it away. It was a gift from my 18 year old son, Matthew. The memory was precious. I decided to keep it. It would be used to hold my bills and create a lasting legacy.

Along with my bills, it will hold my checkbook, a pen, and a calculator. Every Friday morning, I will get the box from off the shelf and sit at the table. I will do the bills and enjoy the process. I will remember the gift from my dear son.

The box will also hold a little pocket Bible. It will be a comfort. It will be a reminder to "do all things to the glory of God."

On the bottom of the box, I will write an inscription - "A gift from Matthew. Mother's Day, May 2011."

Each moment of my life creates a memory. I will make the daily tasks in life more meaningful with a smile, a nod, and a remembrance.

Someday, when the Lord has called me home to heaven, life will go on in my family. They will take on my tasks and continue my work. One of the older children will say, *"We will do what Mother has always done."* Then they will get the Whitman's box. They will sit at the dining room table on Friday morning, and they will open that box. They will pay the bills. They will see my handwritten budget. They will touch the small Bible. And they will continue on the tradition and legacy of their Mother.

6

A Mother's Touch

Many years ago, after my fourth cesarean, I was in tremendous pain. It took me several weeks to recover. Once I started to feel better, I went back to doing what I love best - cleaning, organizing and making a home.

At that time, we lived in a beautiful three story house on the ocean (in Massachusetts). This house was over 100 years old and very elegant. There was a formal dining room with a chandelier and antiques. (We were temporarily renting this house from an elderly couple.) I went in that room first and started to tidy and polish and clean. I set out flowers and place settings on the table. The room looked beautiful. I dimmed the lights, lit a candle and then went in the kitchen to make a special meal. My husband (who was home recovering from a car accident) came into the room. He saw what I had done, and with a sigh of relief and gratefulness, he said quietly... "I got my wife back."

There was a time when I didn't really care about Mother's day or Valentine's day. But as time went on and my children began to grow up, all of a sudden I needed those days. The children get so caught up in their own lives; they don't take the time to show appreciation to their mother. So I had to make these days special. A couple of years ago, I invited my older ones home. They were to bring their boyfriends with them. Here is what I did:

1. I got all dressed up in fancy clothes.

2. We went to church that morning.

3. When we got home, I got right to work on lunch. I laid out refreshments on the table - cheddar cheese, veggies, crackers.

4. I made mashed potatoes, homemade biscuits, BBQ meatloaf, peas, salad and lasagna.

5. There were brownies and ice cream for dessert.

6. The table was set in an elegant way.

Rachel (21) and her boyfriend came with flowers and gifts for me. Nicole (20) and her boyfriend arrived with a large bouquet of flowers and a card. It was such a special day. All the children gave me precious little gifts. My husband gave me flowers too. But what made the day so wonderful is that I worked so hard to make it great. I made a big meal and smiled and laughed and created a precious day for all of them. It wasn't about the flowers or gifts, it was about the wonderful tradition of home and family and food. It was about having a reason or excuse to celebrate.

This is a Mother's touch... This is what makes a home...

Yesterday I walked up to my dear husband and said, "Baby?".....
"If I give you some money, will you buy me flowers and chocolate on your way home from work?" He smiled and agreed. I was

delighted. I thought he would buy me a small box of Whitman's Sampler for $1.00. That's what I suggested. I also thought he would get me some simple carnations for a few dollars. But when he came home, He was so happy to see me. He handed me a dozen roses and a large box of Russel Stover chocolates. What a delight! We went right to work polishing the table and putting the roses into vases. I put on my "homemaking" music (Classical - Canon in D) and the mood was set. It was a Mother's touch.

Home can be the most precious place of all if we put our hearts into it. Despite any trouble that goes on, despite any drama or trials, we need a mother's love to make home a haven.

Mother's Book of Home Economics

7

Afternoon Knitting

After my morning work is done, in the home, I have been happily knitting. I have always wanted to knit a pair of fingerless gloves, but couldn't seem to figure out how. I stumbled onto an easy pattern, perfectly explained. I was delighted. It took me quite some time before I actually started the project, but one pleasant afternoon, I found some yarn in my dressing room and got to work.

At times, I forget basic things, like how to cast on, or bind off. (*Frankly, I am not that bright. - smiles*) I have been grateful for a little helper that has made my knitting time very easy. It is a pretty little book called, "The Knitting Answer Book."

It took me about a week to finish the project. I only knitted during my afternoon homemaking breaks. It was a special time and I enjoyed the work.

Now that the gloves are finished, I need to find another easy project. I want to get out the ironing board and iron pretty material for sewing projects. Maybe I will make a new apron for spring.

I can keep my sewing box handy for the next few months. I will even take it out on my front porch to enjoy the warm sunshine while I hand-sew.

Afternoons are such a peaceful time to begin winding down the day. Most of the work is past; the dinner hour will soon arrive. But that little space of time before the sun sets is perfect for hand projects. One can listen to the quietness of the day, the birds chirping outside, the wind blowing, or even a convicting sermon on CD!

Should Mother Work Outside the Home in 1981?

I am reading a charming old magazine, published in June of 1981. It is called, "The Joyful Woman" and was published by the daughters of the late evangelist, Dr. John R. Rice.

There is an article in here, "*Shall I be Part-Time Worker and Part-Time Mother?*" written by Delores Elaine Bius. It is so interesting. Basically, Mrs. Bius is talking about her confusion over whether or not she should go out and get a job. She is worried about the bills. She has two married sons and three in high school. Her loving husband supports her and loves having her at home. When she approaches the family with her idea of getting a job, her sons discourage her. One says, "Mom, didn't you ever hear of Murphy's Law? It explains that the more money you have coming in the more your wants increase. It's a vicious cycle. Before you knew it, you would change from a part-time job to a full-time one. I think you should forget the idea of working altogether."

Her husband reminds her that "The cattle on the thousand hills are the Lord's." He trusts God for their finances and isn't concerned about the bills. Besides, Mr. Bius is already taking care of them all just fine. His wife is just getting a little pulled into what society around her is doing.

This is such a cute article and fascinating to see what housewives often thought about working in the early 1980's. It ends with this adorable thought:

Mrs. Bius says, "If Satan starts to tempt me again with thoughts of a job outside my home, I will say, 'Get thee behind me.' "

Isn't it interesting to realize this same struggle is still going on today? Should Mom work outside the home or not? Well, according to the Bible, she is to be a Keeper at Home. That is enough for me and I am thrilled to be at home. What an honor!

The Sanctuary of Home

There will always be storms brewing out in the world, for Mothers to *silently* fight. There will be lurkers, with ulterior motives, trying to lure the residents away from a godly home. There will be temptations of events to keep mother so distracted and busy that she doesn't remember how to keep home a quiet place of rest.

- **Mothers must learn to make home a sanctuary**. -

Today, the sporadic holiday traffic out front is bringing sudden and alarming noises. I have a baby here who needs his morning rest. I closed the blinds to keep out the heat of the sun. I closed the front windows to stop the traffic sounds. Then I opened the back windows so we can hear the soothing sound of the rushing water of the back river. Baby will sleep soundly at our quiet Estate.

Sometimes we have to shoo out certain people from rooms in our house, in order that we may keep a *gentle home* running. We may even send loud children outdoors to play. It is good for them, and good for us. Mothers often send guests home when the hour is getting late. The home must have order, and the residents must have their wholesome rest.

Bible time and prayer - hour should be sacred events, which occur at regular times. When Mother is delighted and peaceful and rested, the family will happily follow her in the parlour for the time of worship. It will be almost as awe-inspiring and precious as reading a beautiful bedtime story. The short time of devotion is a time of reverence and holiness. It is a discipline in *consistency* and a lesson in serving the Lord.

When family and guests enter Mother's sanctuary (of a godly home), they should immediately sense her joy and warm welcome. The residents know Mother works hard to make home a pleasant and happy place.

Is this *ideal place* worth fighting for? Is it worth shutting out the world at regular times so the family can enjoy a respite, taking refreshment and rest they dearly need?

When they leave Mother's well - tended sanctuary, will their hearts yearn to be back soon? Will they get homesick for that loving place?

Babies and small children need rest and order and the routine of a *home nursery*. In this fast paced world of overindulging in everything, wouldn't it be worthy if more Mothers created this same type of nursery at home for *all who enter*?

Mother's Book of Home Economics

10

When Ironing Makes it All Better

There are days when housework is dreaded. We are not in the right "mood" to clean and bake and cook. Or, perhaps we are letting some trial take over our mind, causing us to fall into despair. This is sad, because once we start our chores, we are often happy and at peace. There is *joy* in dusting and polishing. There is *pride* in cooking for the family. There is *happiness* in creating a pleasant haven in our homes.

At times like this, one of my favorite things to do is get out the old ironing board. I might get pillowcases and sheets if there is nothing else to iron, but I get something. I can set up the board anywhere in the house. It is nice to be near the children. Or I might turn on an old black and white movie to watch while I work.

Ironing is done in a slow and careful manner. It forces one to be peaceful. This kind of work should not be done in a rush, or under stress; because that would take away its benefits. Of course, the clothes we iron will look lovely, without wrinkles! But the warmth of the iron and the steady movements we make while we work, will bring a calmness over us.

Husband and children will see this. They will see something that is rare in this culture, where sloth and slacking are the goal. Family will see that mother loves home and she loves her housework. She will be with the family and they will see her doing the old homemaking tasks, *the rare tasks that help make home special*, and this will somehow bring peace in the home.

The next time you are not in the mood to clean, or you are overcome by sadness, just get out the ironing board and enjoy a precious task that homemakers have been doing for generations. Trust me, you will feel so much better!

Mother's Book of Home Economics

11

Echoes from the Kitchen

I have been listening to the old songs of Patsy Cline on my kitchen radio while I work. The sound is not as crisp as modern recordings. It adds a sort of nostalgic gentleness to my chores.

While I wash dishes, polish the stove, and sweep, the echoes of Mother's work goes throughout the house. The sounds of the old music tells the family that Mama is busy in the kitchen. It makes them happy to know that, *very soon*, there will be something special to eat, and the kitchen will be clean and polished.

The Echoes from my Kitchen will become a memory for my growing children. They will remember all the work I did in there with love and creativity.

I was talking to Mr. White yesterday about baking pies. He wants a chocolate cream one. I told him I would try my very best to have a different homemade pie, or a special cake, for the family each Sunday afternoon. It will be a new tradition. Thinking of lovely things to do during kitchen time keeps things exciting!

There are many things we can do to make our kitchens *homemade* and special. We need to enjoy being in there. It should be our favorite place in the house. Perhaps some lace curtains or a vintage flower vase would add special homestyle touches. Or maybe a pretty basket for apples or oranges near the breadbox. Whatever pretty things you can find to make your kitchen unique will help you enjoy the work so much more. . . *And the Echoes of your Kitchen work will touch the hearts of all who enter.*

12

Bossy Wives

Many of us nag our husbands. We give them lists of things to do,
just like they are our children. We boss, we control, we irritate.
Perhaps we do this rarely, or without even noticing, but we all do it.
This morning I caught myself "*offering a suggestion*" to my husband
about our van repairs that needed to be done. The look on his face
was one of "*I was already planning to do that, but now I won't
because you told me to!*" After I walked out of the room, I realized
my mistake. I came back and apologized by telling him a joke I'd
seen on the *"I Love Lucy"* show.

Lucy "disappeared," to get attention, by pretending she was
missing. Fred Mertz told Ricky he shouldn't bother replacing his
wife by remarrying. He should just get a parrot to nag and throw
away his money. When I told this to my husband, he laughed. *All
was well.*

When will I ever learn that my husband has his own agenda?
When will I learn that he has his own routine and ways of handling
his duties? Can you just imagine if someone like Grace Kelly tried
nagging Prince Rainier? What if our husbands were Supreme Court
judges or high ranking generals in the army and we wives tried

telling them what to do? Are our own husbands any less important or intelligent?

Do you know what is interesting? Few husbands nag or boss around their wives. So why do *we* do it?

13

Free Presents for Mother

For my birthday this year, I devised a lovely plan that won't cost any money. I gathered my teenagers around and announced, "It's time for a family meeting. . . " *I smiled,* "About my birthday."

They came running.

I told them I wanted something so very much, and said they didn't need to spend a dime.

One of them guessed, "We don't have to clean the house, do we?"

"That's it!" I cheered!

But it will be much more fun than that.

I am putting together a lovely little package and will leave it on my kitchen table. I will use a large shoe box and wrap it up with delicate wrapping paper. I will write on the top, "Happy Birthday Mother!" Then I will put a slot in the top.

Beside this, will be a small basket with a great many index cards. Each card will have the name of a specific chore, such as "dust all the baseboards." There will also be a spot to sign the child's name, and the date the chore was completed. This card will then go into the happy birthday box as a present for mother! (The children will have an entire week to get these done.)

On my actual birthday, I will open the box, read all the cards and thank my loving children. I will then walk the house with great joy and see all the beautiful clean rooms. I can't wait!

14

Chalkboard Prayers

When I really need a miracle, I write my prayer requests on a chalkboard. This is on my living room wall. It is in a "public place." I use this as a serious act of faith and courage, not only for a witness to myself but also to my entire family.

I first started doing this about a year or so ago. I was having trouble finding my notebook, where I normally list my prayers. So I just decided to write a list of major financial needs on the chalkboard. I knew the Lord would take care of these for me.

Well, as I wrote these out, some of the children gathered around and wanted to know what I was doing.

"These are my chalkboard prayers. They are serious problems that only God can fix." I would tell them.

Within a few days, I was able to cross each one off. They were all being taken care of. My Nicole (19 at the time) was amazed. "You have to tell me how you do that!!"

Well, I did it again the other day. I wrote my list. I only write these publicly (in my living room) when the answers will require a miracle. These requests are impossible for me to handle alone.

Anyway, I put up a list the other day. There are currently five items listed there.

Well, this morning, the hardest of all was resolved. It gave me great joy to cross that one off. I was so grateful!! I told all the children.... I told my Father... I told my Mother.... Then I told them they needed to get a chalkboard too, and write up their own prayers.

15

Remembering Suppertime

I came home from shopping late this afternoon. It was 5 p.m. I needed to get supper going. I quickly shooed the children off into the other room. I didn't want help. I wanted to enjoy my kitchen and the art of preparing a meal for my family.

I quickly put on my apron, and carefully laid out the groceries on the table. I put on some sweet, old fashioned gospel music and started getting the stove ready so I could cook. I loved stirring the food, and setting the table. I put out the place settings and put away groceries while supper was cooking. It is so peaceful making a home.

I remember how my mother used to work in her kitchen. We were all doing our homework or watching television. Then we would hear her call for us, "Supper's ready!" Oh, we were so happy! We would race into that kitchen and take our seats. Mom made sure we had fresh vegetables in serving bowls and plenty of bread. Dad would sit at the head of the table. He still had his work uniform on. He was a machine mechanic and I still recall that blue dress shirt and dark pants. Dad would say the most precious prayer and we waited expectantly for him to finish. We always felt like such good children when Daddy prayed. Then we enjoyed talking and visiting while we enjoyed Mother's cooking.

After supper, we children would clean the kitchen while Mom and Dad had coffee in the living room. We felt safe and secure, knowing that each night, Mom would have our dinner ready at 5 p.m. And we knew every one of us would be sitting at that table, eating all together.

Tonight, when I finished cooking, I called down the hall to my children, just like my mother did when I was little, *"Come on, it's supper time."* And as I said those words, tears welled up in my eyes.

I pray supper is a special time every night in your homes.

Mother's Book of Home Economics

Ideas for a Happy Home

Creating a happy home is a fun job. It takes a lot of work and a cheerful attitude. But we need motivation and ideas to keep it up.

Getting Help from Teens

The past few days, as I've been getting my energy back, I didn't want to take on too much housework. So I asked my boys (14 and 19) to do some of my work. They are sweethearts and are willing to help, but my oldest son is busier. I had to come up with creative ways to motivate him to help me. Here is what I did:

I asked him to take the 7:00 pm shift in the kitchen. This would mean doing dishes and straightening up. I asked him for help "in reverse," which means I *pretended* to take his side. This made us both smile. As the time approached, I said, "I really don't want you to nag me, but I know you want me to do the dishes." He smiled, but didn't budge. He was working on a project. When it was just about 7, I went to him again and said, "You know? You have been nagging me all day about those dishes. Can't you see I'm busy? I will try to do them in a minute." He smiled again. I walked away. He did the dishes.

Creating the right Atmosphere

Sometimes, watching old episodes of "The Brady Bunch;" "The Waltons;" or "The Donna Reed show," put me in such a cheerful mood that I want to make my home pleasant and presentable. Other times, I turn on old gospel music, or some Bing Crosby, and I imagine the 1940's housewives and how they kept their homes happy. I have trouble cleaning my kitchen unless a pretty lamp is on, or a candle is lit. I need my surroundings to be pretty and cheerful because that affects my mood.

Reverencing Daddy

I do my best to keep things quiet around the house for Mr. White. I also make sure he has his coffee, clean clothes and clean dishes. I encourage the children to honor their father, by honoring him myself. Many Dads have a special chair where they can relax. Home should be the place these men want to come home to.

Careful with Money

We have to strive for a home- centered attitude, rather than a shopping one. The goal is to avoid unnecessary spending and keeping the focus off finances, on a day-to-day basis. Money is certainly important, but it is not the main part of our daily life. We need to think more on spending time with family, reading, keeping busy with hobbies and our chores.

We also need to keep the bills low, conserve the use of utilities and fuel for the cars. When we are careful with our money, everyone is much happier at home.

Mother's Book of Home Economics

Mother's Attitude

With so many problems facing Mothers, we need to work on having a peaceful attitude. Of course we are going to get upset, and worry about things. If we learn to seriously give things over to the Lord, and not worry about everything, we will have an easier time.

The Daily Fight

To have a happy home is going to take a daily fight. We will fight bad news, irritating people, messes, accidents and sickness. These fights are in the mind. We fight off the negative, and work on remaining steady through it all, *like the hand that does not shake in the midst of trauma.* This takes practice. It sometimes takes a lot of pep talks! But we must remind ourselves daily that we can have a happy home - if we decide it will happen - no matter what may come!

17

Getting Along in Marriage

Stress and trials in daily life can cause fights in marriage. Husband and Wife may argue about money, bills, the condition of the house, or the children. A Husband might be angry with his wife for neglecting what she is supposed to do, while a wife might be angry with her husband for his hostility or mistreatment. All this can be avoided, or lessened, if we use the most important technique in marriage. It is so simple, yet so difficult!

It is all about using social manners. It is common courtesy to show emotional restraint in public. We must avoid creating a "scene" when we are upset. We hold back our frustration and anger for the good of those around us. When a lady acts with such control, she is considered to be dignified and admirable.

We must learn, on a daily basis, no matter how often we are tempted to act otherwise, that we must act with grace in private, just as we would in public.

For those who tend to let their anger erupt and blow off steam to those around them, they must learn, by constant practice, to get control of their emotions. It is extremely selfish to *rant* and *rave* and *insult* and *blame* when we are upset. We cannot allow ourselves to get so angry that we lose our dignity. We must learn good manners.

Getting along in marriage requires the skill of polite communication, no matter the circumstances around us. For a husband and wife to 'fight fair' they should remember a few things:

1. They will have differences of opinions and will annoy each other. Expect this. We are all human and have flaws. Have enough compassion to let these things go.

2. Avoid fighting in front of guests or your children. To fight in front of others is one of the most selfish things we can do. It shows a lack of restraint. It shows a lack of dignity.

3. Never bring up past hurts. It will only prolong a fight and make it more extreme.

4. Remember that it is normal to be upset with others, even those we love, but we should never allow our scathing words to rend the heart. To make it plain - watch your mouth! . . Guard your words!

5. Never, ever, ever talk about your spouse in a negative way to others. Guard the privacy of your home. This is an essential part of good manners.

An example of good manners in marriage reminds me of "The Waltons." The storekeeper's wife referred to her husband as "Mr. Godsey." She only called him by his first name during private moments.

When we wives learn how to use proper communication and emotional restraint in our daily lives, our good manners are observed by our children. They will learn from this. This will affect them for good and not evil. Sadly, in this current "me-centered" society, it will take tremendous effort to practice proper manners in daily life. It will be an ongoing battle with our words and thoughts. But it is worth every bit of effort!

Remember this - a lady will use good manners even when no one else does. She will do this even if there is no reward. She will do this because it is the right thing to do.

The joy of a happy marriage is based on a wife as the center of good morals, virtue and loveliness. This is all clearly seen by her behavior. And it brings a light of beauty into a cold, sad world.

18

A Wife Who Does Not Complain

We all want a peaceful, happy home. The greatest advice I can offer is for a wife to avoid murmuring, mumbling and being discontent.

A wife who does not complain is a *virtuous* asset to her husband.

I was reading about the life of a famous Rabbi, "The Story of The Chofetz Chaim" (from *Artscroll Youth Series.)* He was well known and well respected, even though he did nothing that would be considered great by the world. He lived humbly and simply and devoted his time to the study of Torah and living a godly life. He often said that his success in life was because of his wife, saying, "she was satisfied with dry bread and never asked for nice clothes or beautiful furniture and the like."

How often do we wives wish we had nicer things around us? How often do we sigh and say, *aloud*, that we need prettier, newer clothes? How often do we make our husbands feel as if they are not good enough providers?

If we could only remember that we are pilgrims and strangers on this journey, and stop being so distracted by the glitter of the world around us, perhaps then we will have a true eternal perspective.

19

Mama's Kitchen

My mother used to make such wonderful things for supper. No matter what was happening, we could always count on Mama making a good meal for us in the evening. Here are some of the things she used to make:

1. Mashed potatoes and hamburger over vegetable soup. .. Details: Fry up some ground burger. When this in finished, add one can of Campbells vegetable soup over this. Then add one half a can of water. Stir this up and simmer......... Mash up five pounds of cooked potatoes.... To serve: Put a heaping serving- spoon full of mashed potatoes on a plate. Top with the burger mixture.

2. Spaghetti and meatballs. Mom used to roll up the meat mixture into golf ball size meatballs. She did not fry them. She added them into a pan of tomato sauce and let them cook for hours. She would then top our cooked spaghetti with this. We always had grated Parmesan cheese on the table to sprinkle on top of this delicious meal.

3. At every meal, she would put a plate of bread, a bowl of sliced onions, sliced tomatoes and sliced cucumbers.

4. Mom had serving bowls and plates for everything. Eating was always an event. It was like she was the hostess. We had folded napkins beside our plates, all the silverware we needed and glasses full of milk, iced tea, or lemonade. We *never* had soda with our meals. Soda was a treat we had with a snack once a week.

5. On weekend mornings, Dad would make a big pancake breakfast. Mom was right in there helping him set everything up. We children would sleep as late as we could, but we were awakened by the sound of Dad's gospel music, his singing along, and the delicious smell of breakfast cooking! He made us *want* to get out of bed.

6. Years later, when only two (out of four) of us children were left at home, Dad would get take-out on Friday nights. He would get fish and chips for everyone, except for me. I didn't like fish. So he would make a special trip to Wendy's restaurant and get me a plain hamburger with French fries. We were always excited to see him coming home from work on Friday nights with that special supper!

7. Mom loved to wash dishes. She did them all day long. When we would have a drink in the livingroom on a hot day, she would watch to see when that cup was empty. As soon as we left the room, she would take it and wash it.

8. Mom was always in the kitchen. She would wash down the counters and have the tea kettle on to enjoy a cup of hot tea on her break. To this day, when I go downstairs to visit her (she lives in a small apartment in our house), I can always find her in the kitchen, organizing, planning or just reading the paper at the table, while drinking tea.

Mother's Book of Home Economics

I have learned so many things about home and homemaking from Mama. I grew up cleaning her house and cooking in her kitchen. I used to wash the kitchen floor just for fun..... All these years later, I still love working in my own kitchen. It is the center of our family. I have my mother to thank for this.

20

When Company Comes

I spent much of yesterday morning on little errands and housework. I picked up one of my girls and one of the grandbabies. We did some shopping and came *home*. Most of my children were here yesterday, along with one of their friends. My parlour was neat and tidy and I made a nice lunch of lasagna with sesame Italian bread.

There was chocolate cake and tea for those who wanted a nice afternoon refreshment. Everyone spent time outside, walking the grounds, or playing games indoors. We visited throughout the house and helped take care of baby.

The ones who weren't here, telephoned in their visit. They missed home and wanted to be here. We had a few pictures to look through; and talked of daily life and news.

I cleaned throughout the day, just a few minutes here; a few dishes to wash there; a chair to tuck in; a floor to tidy; and things stayed nice. I did laundry for one of the grown children. (I love when they come home with their laundry!) Then I rested for a few late afternoon hours. Children came into my room and sat with me while I rested and we enjoyed a little Pepsi.

The past few weeks, I have been reading "To Kill a Mockingbird." Aunt Alexandra hosted The Ladies Missionary Society in the family parlour. Southern neighbors would get all dressed up and have a nice meeting. They would talk of needs in distant or local lands, and then it was time for refreshments. Treats and tea were served on pretty trays. This was where young "Scout" learned to be a lady. Perhaps we can have some sort of missionary society in our own homes. What a nice way to have company, when one uses a portion of their visiting time, for noble causes.

When company comes, even if it is mostly family, it feels like a holiday. It is also a lovely time to enjoy being a homemaker. It is the time to feel rewarded for all the hard labor of washing floors, cleaning windows, and dusting furniture. It is a sweet "recital" at the end of a hard week of work, to showcase one's happy home and share a bit of Christian Hospitality.

21

The Gentle Society of Home

In the rush of daily activities, sometimes we forget how calm and gentle home life can be. There are certain things we can do to help us remember. . .

- **We can have special touches in our favorite rooms**. This may be a living room, entryway, or dining room. Little touches of soothing artwork (like pretty flowers, landscapes, English gardens, or elegant families from the "Victorian" or "Romantic" eras.) Nice, quiet background music of classical or gospel would be lovely and soothing.

- **What we wear, and how we look.** There is something I call "*Casual Elegance*." This is whatever makes you feel dressed up, yet comfortable. For me, that is my blue cotton skirt (knee-length), a pretty top and a nice sweater. (All from either J.C. Penny or Macy's - purchased at their annual winter clearance sale, for very little money.) We can also have a classically, elegant hairstyle. This may be a loose updo, or whatever brings out an *aura of old fashioned sweetness* to the look.

- **Setting a neat table for evening refreshments, and turning on a dim lamp** will calm one's nerves, if one remembers to forget the outside world for a time. (This means not to talk about it, or worry about it, for a little while!)

- **Being quiet.** . . We often talk too much, worry too much, think too much, and want to multitask every minute away! Being quiet and content takes effort, but it will bring peace and gentleness to the family.

Every day, we can take little steps of progress to cultivate a gentle society in the home. We must use our creativity and be the light of our homes. This may mean it is always our *own* ideas, and our *own* labor that makes this happen. But this is a beautiful, noble work. . . *to bring gentleness to a home.*

22

A Cheerful and Willing Housekeeper

While doing my daily housework today, I realized something. ....
Whenever I am doing laundry, washing dishes, putting things away,
etc, I often ask one of the children to help me. I might say, "Will you
run downstairs and put these clothes away?" or "Sweep the floor for
me, will you?" Then I head off to do some other bit of cleaning. You
are probably thinking.... That's okay..... Children should help
around the house, right? Yes, but I have an important point here:

1. Housework should not be something we rush to have it over with.

2. Do you realize how little we really have to do in our homes,
relatively speaking, compared to farm housewives of the 1800's?

3. In order to be healthy and fit, we should do as much housework as
we possibly can. Yes, give the children chores, but why ask them to
help you with *yours*? What I mean by this is, it is getting to the point
where whenever a child walks into a room, instead of saying "Hi
sweetie!" I say, "Take out the trash" or "would you clear off the
table?"

Here is what I did after my revelation:

I turned on a CD of classical music and started tidying up my kitchen. I washed down the counters, swept the floor, put away the clutter on the counters and just hummed along with the music. All the windows were open. I could feel a cool breeze while I worked. I carefully folded the clothes in the living room, neatly stacked them in piles and then walked all the way up and down stairs to put these away myself. Our remote phone was not on the hook. I started to call downstairs to Amy (14). I wanted her to bring it to me. Then I remembered the opportunity I had to stay fit, so I walked down there myself and got the phone.

It only took me about an hour to make the house look pleasant and inviting. I looked around and was content. I had worked hard. I had earned my rest. Sitting at the table with a cup of hot tea was a pleasant reward. In Scripture, we are told to work 6 days and then rest on the 7th day. Do you realize how much more we will enjoy that rest if we have actually worked hard to deserve it? Yet, some feel that housework is boring, or drudgery. How can that be? If you adjust your thinking, finding solitude and joy in making your house look lovely; wouldn't you feel better about doing these daily tasks again and again? Each morning I wake up to my kitchen work. I am there to serve my wonderful family. I am going to do it cheerfully. I am going to find ways to make it pleasant for me. I light a scented candle (even in the middle of the day), I turn on some gospel or classical music and the mood is set. Keeping house is an art. We have to learn to enjoy it and stop trying to get out of it. The less we

Mother's Book of Home Economics

do around our precious homes, the more lazy and out of shape we will become. How is that a nice legacy to leave to our children?

If they see you enjoying your work, instead of delegating, they will ponder in their hearts how content and at peace you are at home. They will want that same peace when they are older. Where did I learn this from? The example of my own dear Mother.

23

Do You Love Your Kitchen?

I have fond memories of my mother and grandmother in the kitchen. The old housewives loved their special room. They cleaned and baked and cooked. This was the room where they created treats for guests. Food is very comforting. Mothers of the old days set up their kitchens in a way that showed their personal style.

There are many modern kitchens of today, which seem cold and sterile. They look like they belong in a showroom. Personally, I prefer the old kitchens. I love to see handmade curtains, painted cabinets and pretty decorations on the walls. If there is a space for worn out cookbooks - all the better!

Some of the mothers used to have little TV sets in their kitchens. They would watch a little program while they made the family dinner. Or there would be the sound of a record playing or radio program coming from the living room. Mother would hum along while she cheerily set the table, filled glasses with milk, and baked an apple pie.

The Kitchen must be a place where Mother wants to be. She should put special little touches here and there to make it her favorite room in the house. I have a tall stool in my kitchen. I can sit and chat with one of the children while I peel potatoes or roll out biscuit dough. My health is frail and I need to sit. But I love to be in my kitchen.

Our cabinets are painted a dark sage green. My counter is hunter green with ivy leaves. My curtain is burgundy and dark green with decorative fruit. I have pretty welcome plaques on my walls. There is a red blender on my counter. I have sage green canisters. My floor has rips in the linoleum, but it is clean.

My kitchen is old but beloved.

24

Fighting the Money Seeking Mentality

I've been thinking a lot about material goods. Television is full of nice houses, nice cars, and people spending money on things that seem like necessities. I see people all around me with newer homes, good paying jobs, and cash with which to splurge. I have to shake this all off because that is not my value system.

I crave a spiritual life with fewer possessions. My permanent home is in heaven. I pour all my energy on my children, my husband, and my family, seeking my reward in the next life.

Do you remember when large families and hard work were the norm? Do you remember the Depression-era days when neighbors were neighborly and had time to visit, encourage, and help each other out?

Why are people choosing to have fewer children and more possessions? Why doesn't anyone want to stay at home and focus on building up the family? How often does anyone even read their Bible anymore, or go to Church?

Somewhere along the line, the American Dream spiraled out of control. It is not about being surrounded by fine things. It is about having a HOME and a FAMILY.

I am going to print out some old time pictures and consider all the precious souls being trained to do God's work, who will shun worldly goals. We mothers need to start spending more *joyful* time in daily religious duties and making home a godly culture. We need to be the example of being God's servant and fulfilling His calling on our life to our children. We need to stop being distracted by the glitz and glamour of our society.

This week, I am going to pull out all my old Depression-era books and I am going to read and study about the old days. I am going to be inspired by the Old Time Mothers and their godly wisdom. And I am going to wage a war, in my heart, against seeking an abundance of money, which is the ultimate enemy of *trust* and *faith* in an omnipotent God.

25

The Lesson of a *Set–Apart* Life

When my oldest child, Rachel (now 25) was learning to bake as a young girl, we would sit together in the kitchen. I taught her a Jewish custom about making sure the eggs were Kosher. This has great significance, and I will explain what we did:

There were two bowls. We would crack an egg into the smaller bowl and make sure it was "Kosher." Then we would add it to the main bowl. We would continue to do this with all the eggs. If we found any spots of blood, we would discard that egg. Those eggs were not Kosher. The blood is life. Once the blood begins to appear on an egg, it meant that life had begun. We were not to eat the blood with the egg. Was this a difficult process? Of course.

But as we carefully and slowly checked each egg, we made the extra effort, *a set-apart effort*, to follow one of God's precious Laws.

Rachel would look with awe and wonder as we worked. She would always make sure the eggs were Kosher before she began to cook or bake. I remember when she moved into her own home and began to cook without my supervision. She had her own kitchen and her own way. But she continued to make sure her eggs were Kosher, even though her guests would question her. It didn't matter. She would proudly explain what she was doing. She would pass on the law of a set-apart life.

Have you ever seen the episode on "Little House on the Prairie," called "The Craftsman?" This is about an elderly Jewish man who teaches Albert his craft of working with wood and making caskets. Through his daily life and work, he taught Albert the joy and blessing of a set-apart life. It certainly takes more effort. It certainly takes more thought, but it fills the soul with contentment and gratefulness as we acknowledge God in everything we do.

Lovely Work at Home

It is raining and pleasant this early morning. The lush Vermont landscape is inspiring. It makes one want to shut off all technology and enjoy the pleasant tasks of homemaking.

I will sweep and polish by lamplight in my old country kitchen. Our little homeschool will start in just a few minutes. While my teenage student is working on math, I will do some baking as I listen to the rain falling and the birds singing.

I will do a little laundry and delight in the folding and the sorting. It is lovely to put out fresh towels and do those little touches that make this place a home.

I will set the table for the noon meal and have it ready hours before it is needed. This will inspire me to take my time and create an atmosphere of a happy kitchen!

Perhaps I will wash the kitchen floor before enjoying an afternoon rest. I plan to drink hot tea, and read some Amish fiction before getting back to work in the cool of the day.

A Good Little Housewife

Have you ever started your spring cleaning with a happy attitude? Even getting all dressed up and putting on a pretty apron to help set some ambiance in the home? We can listen to classical music or old time gospel and enjoy the task of heavy cleaning. One feels like **"a good little housewife"** as one takes pride in one's efforts and delights in the work of making and keeping a lovely home. The housewife can sense the gratefulness and happiness as her husband *trusts her* with all pertaining to home and family.

In today's society, housewifery is still being scoffed at by those who choose another path. I cannot imagine why. It is a precious way of life and something to aspire to. Years ago, there was a club for girls called, "Future Homemakers of America." I wonder if they are still in operation?

To be called a "housewife" is an honor. It is more long term than "a stay-at-home-mom," because a housewife is considered a married woman who keeps the home. She keeps the home fires burning. She is the hostess of the domestic arts. *She stays at home whether or not she has children*, and she does a marvelous job of setting a happy tone for those who dwell there.

The lady of the house is the pride of her husband and the comfort of her children. Home for her is a life-long career, hobby and occupation. These dear women seek no applause. They seek not fame. The godly housewives of today are the quiet heroes of their communities.

28

When Groceries are the Presents

When I do the grocery shopping, I always buy a few special items for Mr. White. Perhaps it is the ingredients for beef stew. Or, maybe it is a brownie mix. I like to find his favorite things and make them for him at home. He greatly appreciates my efforts.

Of course, I must remember the basics, like coffee and sugar and bread. If we run out of those items, I am slacking on my job. (gentle smiles) But for me to buy those special items, the ones that take extra effort from me, and are bought economically. . . are what make Mr. White happy.

As for me, I am not the type of girl who likes jewelry, a new car, or expensive clothes. Mr. White knows this. When he wants to surprise me, or make me happy, he will buy my favorite frozen pizza (Freschetta), or some Ginger ale. . . Perhaps he will buy me a large bag of m and m's, or some mint-chocolate-chip ice cream. And with these little presents, I am *delighted.*

At different times, each of us will be in the store, looking through the aisles, thinking about what the other would like.

My favorite thing, is to hear him coming home, rattling his pockets, and saying, "I bought you some m and m's!"

And he loves when I come home, put down the grocery bags, and tell him, "I bought you a special kind of burger!"

No fancy restaurant dinner. . . no wrapped presents . . . no trip to foreign lands. . . no night out on the town. . . no.... none of these things can compare to when Mr. White and I buy groceries for presents.

29

Cooking for Mister

I have this old 1963 cookbook published by Better Homes and Gardens.* It has a section in the front called, **"Meals Men Like."** The introduction says:

"Fix any of these delicious meals for your man and you'll be the 'Best Cook' he knows."

A sample menu:

"Stew Supper Supreme"

Old-time Beef Stew

Crisp Cabbage Slaw

Bread Butter

Apple Betty Pie

Coffee Cream and Sugar

The directions suggest serving the pie with vanilla ice cream! The description for the stew says it will serve "6 to 8 hungry folks" and a "*go-with*" would include "thick slices of bread."

It sounds like a delicious meal! Sometimes, when we create a little menu, it makes the experience extra special.

How many housewives today are making a real old fashioned supper for their husbands? How many of us dress up nicely for when he comes home from work, and make his environment peaceful? Certainly it is difficult when we have small children, but even if we did some of our cooking early in the day we could heat it up in the evening.

Cooking for Mister. . . When a wife makes pleasant, home cooked meals and serves them cheerfully, that man will be eager to leave work and head back to his family. It's like he has his own little restaurant, at the greatest place on earth - HOME!

* The Cookbook is called, "So Good Meals."

30

1894 Advice for Housewives

The Following is taken from a book, "*Primer of Domestic Economy*," by Edith A. Barnett.

This was published in London, in 1894:

1. "Whether the income be small or large, certain or uncertain, the good housewife will keep an accurate account of her income and expenditure.

2. To buy on credit is never economical. Shopkeepers naturally ask more when they have to wait for their money.

3. To have a bill at every shop you deal with is extremely harassing, and makes a housekeeper always feel short of money, since every quarter-day she must settle up her debts and then run in debt again at once.

4. The secret of economical buying is never to buy anything that you do not really need, and not then unless you can spare the money to pay for it at once.

5. A penny saved is a penny got.

6. The pennies saved every day by good management, soon become pounds, and what is wanted is to keep them safe against a rainy day;

which is an expression used to signify a time when your income may be less than it is now or some emergency when you may require a little extra expenditure, such as a doctor's bill, or a country trip, or special teaching for a talented and industrious child. Then, again, there is always old age to look forward to, and if that is not already provided for in other ways, some saving should be specially ordained to meet it.

7. Probably women as housekeepers spend the greater part of the money that is spent in the world."

31

The Thrifty Kitchen

Must the cookie jar always be full? Do Mothers have to keep a steady supply of cake, brownies and other treats in the kitchen? Must she provide her family with gourmet dinners each night, or special meals that taste delightful?

Or is it okay to have a thrifty kitchen? This kind of kitchen produces things like oatmeal in the morning, or whole grain apple muffins. Lunches might be sandwiches or leftovers. Supper might be the main meal of the day, served around 5 or 6 in the evening. This could be pasta, meatloaf, or one of our frugal favorites, southern cornbread, home fried potatoes and baked beans.

It is not required that Mother buy soda, candy or chips. It is completely unnecessary for her to serve dessert every single day. It is also extremely expensive.

Simple, homemade foods from the kitchen help keep household expenses low.

It has been said that we must not be fashionably dressed *above our means*. It is also true that we must not grocery *shop* and *cook* beyond what we can afford.

One of the biggest leaks in the family budget is an abundance of food.

Here are some ideas for keeping costs down:

1. Have meals at specific times, whenever possible. This way everyone knows what to expect. It also helps Mother plan her day. (For example - Breakfast at 8 a.m. Lunch at noon. Dinner at 5 p.m.)

2. Have basic foods in the pantry - like potatoes, vegetables, fruit, flour, sugar, cornmeal, and meat. This way you can quickly come up with something to make, without worrying about rushing off to the store.

3. I know many people write up weekly menus and meal plans, but it is not always necessary if you have basic ingredients available. You should also have some basic family recipes handy that are easy, quick, and frugal.

4. Make special foods, like cookies, once a week. This is something the family will look forward to and appreciate. It could be a Friday night treat. Or, plan on making a cake or nice dessert for Sunday afternoons. The less often treats are offered, the less likely money will be wasted.

5. Offer children basic beverages like juice, tea, water or milk. If the older ones want soda, or some name brand drink, *have them use their own money.* (Mother is not obligated to provide the children with commercially prepared, designer beverages.) This goes the same for candy bars and other processed snacks.

6. Serve whole grains and fresh foods. This is nutritious and helps keep everyone feeling full.

7. In restaurants, patrons are served ice water before their meal. This helps fill them up. Try this at home! Why? Because in this current day, people tend to eat much larger portions than they really need. If they have some water first, they will eat a more appropriate amount of food.

8. Some nutritious snacks include: crackers with peanut butter; celery with cream cheese; sliced apples; carrot sticks; or wheat crackers with cheese. (*Not donuts, danishes, or cupcakes.*)

I realize it takes a tremendous amount of work to have a thrifty kitchen. It is much easier to buy convenience foods. However, there is more at stake than just saving *time* or *money*. We need to save our health.

32

Industrious at Home

There is a lot of confusion about what goes on in an average home. Modern families are distracted by television, home theaters, video games and the features of cell phones. Sometimes, we are so busy with these types of entertainment, we forget what it is like to be industrious at home.

A day may start with opening drapes and shades. There might be a time of morning Bible reading - a *little chapel* in the quiet seclusion of home. Next, some housework is started. Perhaps tidying up the rooms, starting laundry, and then beginning a simple meal of breakfast to serve in a formal- sort- of- way at the kitchen table. Do people still put salt and pepper or cream and sugar on the table, to share a meal with loved ones? Or does everyone grab food and run?

The mid morning hours are for general housekeeping. We clean the kitchen, dust, vacuum and straighten beds. Once the house is in order, it may be time to sit and take a little break. Perhaps it is tea time? Or maybe time to chat and visit with the ones at home, while doing some knitting, embroidery, mending, or sewing?

Lunch hour is like opening a *little cafe* for a time. Some homemade food is prepared and lovingly served at the table. We take

Mother's Book of Home Economics

a break from our home labors and join together for the noon meal. A prayer over the meal begins the time of fellowship.

Before long, some may need a time of rest. Little ones are off to their naps after some time outdoors in the fresh air. This break is helpful to prepare for the afternoon and coming evening.

Dinner is usually started in the early afternoon. Some have helpers at home, while other homemakers do the work alone. It is an exciting time - deciding what to make for the family's evening meal!

While food is baking in the oven, or simmering on the stove, we may find some time for reading and sipping on tea. My mother-in-law always had fresh coffee, which she enjoyed throughout the day. We may do some last minute cleaning, finishing up the laundry, tidying rooms, and cleaning up the kitchen as we work at a more leisurely pace.

Just before the dinner hour, it is time to wind down the day. Sometimes guests stop by to visit. We enjoy their company while we continue our industry. If they arrive at a time when we can take a break, we may serve a little cake and tea and delight in the joy of being home.

Soon the family is seated at the table. Prayers are said. Conversation is started and the meal is enjoyed by all. This relaxing time of eating together at a formal dinner, with napkins, and salt and pepper placed in the center of the table, is a delight.

At this dinner table, and throughout the day, no one is secretly texting a friend. No one is rushing off to play video games. No one is talking about the television program they are missing out on. No one is ignoring the family by endless phone or computer conversations. Why? *Because none of those things have been invented yet . . . in this little home of industry.*

The evening hour has come. It is time to gather for family prayers and Bible reading. Everyone has a bedtime. There is order and structure. Everyone knows what is expected and they yield happily. Once the day is finished, we look back and think what was done in this house that is anything special? What was done that was industrious?

This home was full of service and love and old time family values. This type of home is priceless! The residents in this place, and the goings on there, will have a tremendous influence for generations to come. We just need Homemakers willing to continue the tradition of being industrious at home.

33

A Dangerous Mood for a Housewife

I woke up very cold this morning. The wood stove has gone out. I am not depressed, but feeling unmotivated. This is a dangerous mood for a housewife. My family needs me to be cheerful and happy. They need to see me loving my daily tasks, because I do them for my children. I want their childhoods to be filled with good memories and their hearts must love home.

Dear God, help me to "wake up" from this sloth of the mind!!!!

I will put on my apron, have a hot cup of tea and just start my morning routine. The action will help bring the right thoughts. I cannot sit in a chair until I "feel" like doing my housework. (shudder). I must get up and begin making home our haven of rest. It has to be a place of joy and peace. May God protect me from my own mood!

I will offer myself a reward. . . Once I get everything clean and neat, I will watch a nice movie from the old days. I will think of horse-drawn carriages, Victorian homes, hospitality, and serving tea and cakes.

Perhaps, I will even set a pretty table at the noon hour and serve a simple meal. I will use paper place cards. I can use my neatest handwriting and carefully write out each name with a heart. I will then put one at each place setting. This always makes the family smile. I do it rarely, but it is such a treat.

May there be peace and joy in your homes today.

34

Keeping House

There is a sweet, freshness to the Vermont air. I have all the windows open. I love the sound of chirping birds, and the rushing of the river out back. Each day, I have been doing some little project around the house. Yesterday, I tidied up my dressing room. Today, I will work on the porch and rooms on the first floor, of this 14 room house. We may be having company this weekend so I want to freshen up the rooms. I will have one of my teenagers sweep the porches and do a little weeding of the front grounds.

I have been doing my homemaking in the morning, at a leisurely pace, and then spending my afternoons resting with a book or an old movie. Throughout my day, I take care of the family, especially *grandbaby*, who delights us all with his presence.

Amy (18) has been making most of our meals. She has been a great help, and is a wonderful mother to my little grandson. They have been our house guests for a long time, while her husband is away. It has been a precious blessing!

I love to have a house full of people. I love to watch all the things they like to do, here at the estate. Some sit by a fire, near the tent, toasting marshmallows and chatting. Others play basketball, croquet, or toss around a football. In the late afternoon, my boys (16 and 20)

Mother's Book of Home Economics

can be found in one of the rooms watching a movie. Amy and I love to call the family together at the dinner hour.

My work at home, as a housewife and mother, is to provide a pleasant place of comfort for our family and guests. In order to do this, I have to keep myself pleasant and well rested, by not taking on any activities or outside projects that wear out my mind and strength. *I am grateful for Mister for making this happy home possible, by his work out in the world.*

35

Mother's Home Cooking

In my shopping bag were familiar name brands of groceries. I had *Campbells* soup, *Tony's* Pizza, *Keebler* cookies, and *Kraft* Macaroni and Cheese. I was waiting for someone, and just thinking. Then I realized that I had just bought *convenience foods* that took little effort to make. While this is common in this modern day, it takes away the joy of enjoying Mother's home cooking. If I had just bought some flour, sauce, cheese, chocolate chips, pasta and vegetables, I could have most of the ingredients I needed to make these foods *myself.*

Something is missing in my home, when my husband and children are more excited to see a bag full of name brand foods, rather than being excited when I serve them a delicious homemade supper.

Have I really paid the convenience food industry to take away one of the most precious jobs of motherhood and wifehood? That of being the one to bring joy to the home by my home cooking?

Have you ever heard of travelers who eat in restaurants and diners yet dream about sitting in the kitchen of a traditional home and just having a good home cooked meal? Can that even be found anymore in this day?

In my old cookbooks from the 1960's, there are sections with wonderful advice for the home cook. There are tips and tricks and detailed instructions which teach any aspiring cook how to make a good meal herself. With practice and time and a lot of *patience*, most homemakers can get back to the old arts of cooking. These homemakers can *take back the kitchen!*

This will bring better health to our families, joy to their hearts, and a better quality of life. This will also create a bond and tighten the love and happiness at home. Much money will be saved when mother cooks her own foods. Children and husband will also have appreciation and gratefulness for the sweet lady in the kitchen who (gladly and willingly) takes **time** and *effort* to prepare their food.

Many years ago, when frozen dinners and convenience foods were introduced to the general public, skilled housewives thought it was an *insult* and refused to buy such things! How lovely it would be to have that same pride and capableness of taking on the joyous task of doing our own home cooking!

36

Prayers Which Cannot Be Uttered

When my children were very young, we watched a program on VHS called, "*Shalom Shabbat*." It was adorable and starred Topol (from "*Fiddler on the Roof*"). He was an older gentleman who visited a school to celebrate the Sabbath with the students. He was able to enjoy the Sabbath meal with one of the families. There are a variety of segments, which show us the different foods served in different countries and cultures. There are also very short and precious stories using "clay type - cartoon" people. It was a delightful program.

One segment that struck me was this little boy, sitting on the synagogue steps. There were Hebrew letters all around him and he was puzzled. The Rabbi, on his way into the synagogue, noticed the boy and his dilemma. He announced to the congregation that the service would be delayed. He told them about the young boy, saying that time was needed for the letters to reach heaven and form into a prayer.

Sometimes, in our own prayer life, we don't always know what to say. At other times, we may be so overcome by the trials and pain in our lives, that a prayer is agonizing and exhausting. What this boy and Rabbi teach us is that we don't always have to *say something* in our prayers. There are times we are so weary and dumbfounded, that it is a precious blessing to just sit at the Master's feet, *mute*, and be comforted. God knows what we would have said, or what we need. *He understands*.

37

Mother's Benevolent Society

One of the greatest opportunities for the homemaker is her charitable acts within the home. If she can only delight in her calling, and lot in life, she can become a bright light of good deeds, noble virtue, and kindness to her family.

Sometimes when I would teach my children to do some little service, or help, for their siblings, they would perhaps frown or start to complain. I would smile knowingly and say something like, "this will be a *mitzvah*. It is a good deed, following the principles and commandments given by God, and He will reward you for it. It is *His* work you are doing." The term "mitzvah" was taught to my children when they were very young. It is a Jewish term which is a keeping of the many commandments of God. It has also been said that by doing a mitzvah, a bond is created by God and man. There is a joy in it, a loving service for *the Lord above,* and that makes it precious.

While we mothers are not always in the sweetest, holiest of moods, our main goal is to be kind hearted, and warmed by the presence of God. This will pour through us, in our own actions and words. In this way we are teaching our children the beauty of a life devoted to benevolence.

But what of the Mother's own actions?

It is very easy to become overwhelmed and even annoyed with all the work heaped upon us. It almost becomes a burden and a tremendous pressure that may crush us down if we let it. Yielding to this work with a sweet temper is a herculean task. It cannot be done instantly. It cannot even be done in our own strength. But if we pray and read our Bibles, and sing our hymns and spend time in the holy worship of the Lord, He will give us the strength we need to do HIS work. . . The main problem of yielding to our tasks is that we take on far more than we are capable of doing. We often burden ourselves with impossible expectations and we all suffer because of it.

There is a simplicity in running a society of benevolence in the home. There are basic tasks, and loving service, and little chores. This slow-paced work should not be done in a hurry or under pressure. These tasks should be done *as unto the Lord.* The work can be done as many mitzvahs, with prayers and praises that continue to create a moment-by-moment bond to God. This will bring us great peace and great joy that will fill us with a charitable, loving demeanor. All who observe this, all who are the beneficiaries of this, will be warmed by this light and will carry on for us, and with us, for as long as we are in this society.

Mother, will you become a member of the benevolent society? Will you set one up in your own home? Will your influence and example affect your family and those around you with the beauty of holiness?

We must all remember this the next time a child whines; a dish is broken; the trash needs to be removed; someone is cranky; and when everyone forgets to do their own work. We must remember to face these supposed burdens with a new excitement of doing mitzvahs and being charitable to those who have been placed in our care - including our guests, our children and our husbands.

Mother's Book of Home Economics

38

The Skilled Housewife

Keeping house is more than just doing dishes, or ironing clothes. It is more than fixing supper or washing floors. Being a housewife is a skilled profession. In the old days, girls took home economics courses in school. Some even went to college to study the science of homemaking. It is a beautiful thing to see a lovely, *cared for* home, even if there are humble surroundings.

Housewives need to learn the art of cooking, baking, sewing, mending, decorating, cleaning, thrift and so much more. They need to take pride in their work, putting forth their best effort.

The other night I was washing the dishes, while listening to *Crooners* on the radio. I thought of how there are so many people who hate their jobs, and I was thankful that I loved mine. I love being here. I am grateful for the training I've had, and the experience I have in homemaking. I delight in setting an atmosphere of "home" for all who enter.

I took 3 years of home economics in school. I also studied for four years as a secretary, which taught me how to be a helper and assistant to my husband. It also taught me how to manage books and keep things organized and efficient. I worked as a maid and spent much of my time taking care of children. All this happened before I turned 18 years old. I was *taught* how to keep house. I was *trained* in the art of homemaking and motherhood. For this I am eternally grateful.

39

Manners Learned at the Finishing School

I attended a *homemade* finishing school. This was conducted a few times a month with the assistance of my Aunt. She lived in a lovely house a few streets over from us. Her house was decorated with elegant paintings, beautiful lamps and lovely furniture. She had a guest room with white bedroom furniture, a rose colored lamp, end-tables and gorgeous shades on the windows. There was even a large vanity mirror above the dresser.

My sister and I were invited to sleep over her house. She would set our hair in rollers, then settle us in the guest room. She would open the door just a bit, and say, "*Do you girls need anything?*" We were so comfortable in the soft beds, and warm, expensive blankets, that we felt like royalty. She was an excellent, patient hostess. I never saw her rushing about.

In the morning, we would get all dressed up and go out to breakfast. The first restaurant I remember was across from the harbor in a lovely Massachusetts town. Auntie taught us how to sit up straight, order our food, and place a napkin on our laps. She told us which silverware to use and how to act like ladies. This was all done as if there was all the time in the world.

This went on for many years. Then, as we got older and started to move on, we girls were busier and didn't have much time for our "informal" lessons. My sister and I had a different schedule. We weren't together as often. On occasion, as I was walking to the high school bus stop, in the early morning hours, my Aunt would be on her way to work. She would stop and pick me up. This was the first time in my life I ever heard classical music. It was calming and soothing. She would listen to this on her way to the city, where she would take the subway, or ferry, into Boston for the day's work.

At other times, she would invite me to breakfast. My favorite place was called "Mug 'n Muffin," which was a high class cafe in the plaza. The lights were dim. The tables were dark mahogany, and the booths were burgundy leather. I always ordered the same thing - A hot chocolate with whipped cream, and a warm chocolate chip muffin served on a delicate plate. I ate this with a fork, as if it was a delicious pastry one could order in a French restaurant. During our little visit in the cafe, we would talk about our days and upcoming plans.

Auntie had family parties at her house. We always dressed up for these. She had a finished basement, where a table was set up with a tablecloth. There were all kinds of wonderful things to eat and drink lined up for the guests. It was always family, and perhaps a friend or two. We enjoyed these gatherings so much! We would walk throughout the house, visiting everyone in the different rooms depending on who was where. Perhaps a cousin was in the formal living room. Or, an Uncle in the kitchen talking to Dad and Mom.

Mother's Book of Home Economics

There were usually a few small children who entertained us with their antics. But even they were dressed in their best!

Auntie had stories of travelling. I was most fascinated with her trip to Italy. She once gave me a gorgeous pair of white, long leather gloves which she bought while abroad. I cherish them!

And while this all might sound even more interesting when reminiscing, it was really just we girls, spending time with our Aunt through our growing up years. I don't think she even realized she was the very source of our education in manners, or that she was our teacher in a homemade finishing school.

40

Keeping House with Small Children

There are times when keeping house is more difficult. When you have babies and small children, there is not as much time to get everything accomplished. I want to share a few ideas with you:

1. Playpens.

When my children were little, they were always in a playpen. They were taken out for a walk in the fresh air, or to spend time with mother and daddy at certain intervals throughout the day. But all their toys were in that playpen. It was intended to keep them safe. It's strange now that experts tell us to let the babies run free and explore. But this is so dangerous and makes a mother exhausted.

If I was in the kitchen cleaning or making supper, I would bring the playpen with me, so I could watch my toddler and talk to her, and make her laugh while I worked.

If I was tired and needed a break, I would set up her playpen right beside the couch where I could lay down and she could still reach out to me (or throw toys at me, or hit me on the head with a brush!).

The children loved to watch me vacuum while they giggled from the playpen.

Here is the problem - if your baby is not used to a playpen, good luck trying to get him to stay in one! It should be started from day-one. It should be a normal rule. Once that rule is broken, baby will expect to have all the freedom in the world and will not be content in that safe little playpen.

I want to mention Pilgrim mothers and Colonial mothers. These women cooked over an open fire in their small homes. It would have been fatal to allow a child to roam free. The children were kept in little beds or highchairs, and strapped in their seats while Mama worked, for their own safety. Then they were taken out to get the air, or enjoy the sunshine or play with the family. But they knew they had to be in those seats or beds and played there, quite content, since they knew no other way.

2. When baby is sick.

There will be times when all mother can do is rock the child or pace while holding a sick baby. Those are rough times and very little housework will get done. If possible, see if you can get paper plates, paper cups and frozen dinners. Do the best you can to get by until baby is better.

3. Rules for preschoolers.

My children were only allowed in certain rooms. They were not allowed in my kitchen. I hear stories of preschoolers and toddlers getting into the fridge and helping themselves to snacks. But if they are not allowed in there to begin with, this kind of thing will rarely, if ever, happen. But these rules have to be enforced from day one. A child will never know what he is missing out on, if he is not allowed to do something in the first place.

I remember when Rachel (now 25) and Nicole (24) were little girls. Rachel was 3 and Nicole was 2. They played in our large living room. One day I was cooking in the kitchen and then I walked over to the window. I noticed the girls were giggling and having a wonderful time. They could not see me. Here is what they were doing:

Nicole had her little foot on the Living room rug. But the rest of her body was in the kitchen. She knew she wasn't allowed in the kitchen, so she kept her foot on that rug! She was throwing a toy to see how far it would go into the kitchen and then giggling while she tried to retrieve it. I watched her do this over and over again and that little foot of hers never left the living room rug! Believe me, children will find a way to have a good time and keep the rules at the same time!

No food was allowed in the living room. This was also one of our rules. I remember when I had all five children and we were living in a different home. Amy was 3 years old. She was eating a cracker and then started to walk in the living room. We were all in there sitting and playing. One of the older children scolded her, saying, "**Amy**!! No food in the living room!" That little darling, immediately turned around, threw the cracker back in the kitchen and went on to the living room as if nothing had happened!

4. In the Nursery Stage.

The rules for babies, toddlers and preschoolers should be enforced while they are in the "nursery stage." When they get older and can be trusted with responsibility, it is time to allow them into the kitchen to help with dishes and cleaning. They will feel grown up and needed if they wait until they reach the age of maturity before being allowed in those "grown up" rooms. These "big kids" can also help with the younger ones. They will feel so special when they are finally allowed out of the nursery!

Well, I hope you enjoy the time you have with your little treasures. I know they are messy and loud. I know they don't let you sleep. But do the best you can, and leave the rest!

41

The Maid Was Here

I woke up cheerful and happy this morning. It is a beautiful day. I put on my cutest outfit - A skirt, heels, apron, etc. and got to work. I have a radio in my kitchen. I turned on a cassette tape of some old-southern gospel music and enjoyed tidying my kitchen. I started to remember my work as a maid when I was a teenager. We would go into a house and methodically clean an entire house in 2 hours. These were gorgeous houses in nice neighborhoods. I loved cleaning those homes. But you see, they were not dirty! Everything was clean when we got there. Our job was not to get rid of clutter, or wash dishes. We did not have to remove carpet stains or wash windows. Our job was simply to do the basic deep cleaning, once a week, in order to maintain a house.

Here is what we did:

Kitchen-

Wash sinks and counters. Polish the outside of appliances (stove, fridge, toaster oven, coffee maker, dishwasher). Polish table and chairs. Wash the floor.

Mother's Book of Home Economics

Bathroom -

Scrub tub, toilet, sink, vanity. Wash mirrors. Wash the floor.
Straighten towels. Fold the toilet paper. (This was a triangle shape at
the edge of the paper roll, facing out - it left a message to say - *the
maid was here*.)

Bedrooms-

Dust and polish all furniture. Make beds or change sheets (if these
were left out for us to do). (We would fold, and tuck in, the ends of
pillow cases just like they do in hotels.) Vacuum carpet.

Hallway -

Vacuum carpet.

Living room / Den / Sunroom, etc -

Dust, vacuum.

The very last thing we did was vacuum the living room carpet, as
we backed out of the room. You could see neat lines in the carpet
and no footprints. (This was another sign to say - *the maid was
here*.)

So this morning, as I cleaned my kitchen and bathroom, I
remembered my days as a maid (from the ages of 15 - 17). I loved
my job. I loved cleaning. To have an orderly, neat home, is such a
blessing. When I finished my housework this morning, I could

Mother's Book of Home Economics

almost sense the cheerful "rainbows" which came from the awe and wonder of a tidy house. I walked out of the rooms, and nodded my head in approval and thought - *The Maid was Here.*

Mother's Book of Home Economics

42

The 15 - Minute Cleaning Helper

I like to be fair about chores. When my children were little, they were each assigned certain tasks each day. One was The Breakfast Hostess. Another was in charge of cooking supper. And another had to keep the living room clean. Each of my 5 children had specific work to do each day.

When I was growing up, our heavy cleaning happened on Saturday. I was responsible for cleaning the bathtub, sweeping down the porch stairs and dusting the living room. I also had daily responsibilities. But each of these jobs, divided between family members, kept our house fairly neat and tidy.

No house is going to be clean all the time. We will always have chores. We will always need to prepare food, clean our clothes, and sweep. But things can be kept decent when we have helpers.

As children get older, they have more outside activities and projects going on. They are also less likely to *want* to hang around with Mom (smiles) and do housework all day. So yesterday, I decided to call my teenage son over and tell him I needed him for just 15 minutes. This was extra work, over and above his normal daily chores.

I set the timer, and we worked quickly. He helped me sort old clothes, throw out extra clutter, do some laundry, and deep clean our dish-drainer. I was delighted with the extra help and was happy to get a few piled up things accomplished.

Today, I plan to have another 15 minute cleaning burst with some of the children. It makes things more fun. I have a list of things I want cleaned and will put it on the kitchen table. Each of us can pick and choose what we want to do. Once the work is finished, we are to put a check mark next to the job and then write down our initials (so we know who did what). When I tried this stunt recently, my son did far more work than I did, and was *gloating*.

Another thing I like to do is have cleaning contests with my grown daughter. (She lives 2 hours away from me.) We call each other on the phone and then talk about what we are dreading for overdue housework. Today, we decided to deep clean our bathrooms. I am supposed to call her this afternoon and discuss our progress. However, I had some extra energy early this morning and already finished!

Finding creative ways to make housework fun is one of the greatest things we can do as mothers.

Mother's Book of Home Economics

43

Memories of Ironing and Other Chores

When I was growing up, we lived in a large house in Massachusetts. I remember getting myself up in the morning to get ready for school. I would get one of my skirts and tops and set up the ironing board. We had this charming side porch on the second floor. It was all enclosed and had lots of windows.

I could look out and see the boats going by and enjoy the bright morning sunshine. I would start ironing my clothes. I thought about my plans for the day while I worked. In front of me, would be the single French door that led into our living room. Beyond that was our old piano and a china cabinet. We had simple, cozy furniture and a large throw rug over a linoleum floor.

I would think about cleaning the house while I ironed. The more I worked around the house, alone with my happy thoughts, the more I wanted to clean and make things look nice.

I took home economics classes in school. I loved to cook and bake and sew and clean. Some days I would call my mother from a payphone at school and make her a deal. I would say, *"If you let me leave school early, I will come home and clean."* She always agreed. It wasn't that she needed me to clean. The house was *already* clean. She also loved to clean too. But she knew that I needed a mental break from my troubles. I needed to go home and work on the home arts to survive! I always felt better after washing the floors, or folding laundry in the comfort of that lovely childhood home.

This must be why I love housework, even to this very day. I have tried to teach it to my children. I will not know the results of my efforts until they have homes of their own. But I hope I have passed on a love of home and a love of keeping things pleasant and neat.

"The ordinary acts we practice every day at home are of more importance to the soul than their simplicity might suggest." - Thomas Moore

Mother's Book of Home Economics

44

The Visiting Hour

In the old days, company would stop by to visit on the weekends or early evenings. They would often see the family in the yard, or garden, and know it would be okay to come by. Neighbors and friends would visit on the porch, or by the fence. Sometimes, they were invited into the house for a piece of pie or for lemonade.

These kind guests would not overstay their welcome. They would even visit while helping fix a car, or hanging the wash onto the line. When the dinner hour would arrive, they would leave the family to their routine and quiet time and head to their own home. If a lady visited a housewife, she knew to leave before (or right when) the husband arrived home. She knew he needed a quiet rest.

Relatives were known to visit at all hours and that was expected. But friends and neighbors had a more limited access to one's life.

Today, it is uncommon to see people sitting on their porches or out in their yards for long periods of time. In Northern New England, here in the U.S, folks are not as friendly as they are in the South. You don't see people waving to strangers as they drive, or walk by. New Englanders feel a coldness rather than a friendly welcome. This makes it harder to find an opportunity to visit.

Many people are indoors watching television, using computers or playing video games. This sort of recreation has taken away some of the outdoor time (or visiting time) which used to be available.

I wonder if there is a way to spread a nationwide time for visiting. I would call it "The Visiting Hour." Perhaps it would be on Saturday afternoons from one to three. This would encourage people to spruce up their homes, have pleasant refreshments to share and welcome a visit from friends and neighbors. It would be an open house time. This can be held on the front porch, with lovely patio furniture, or indoors near the fire. Guests could come and go throughout the few hours. These could be people from church, a neighbor, or a friend from the next county. It would be the national visiting hour and it would be a lovely way to bring communities together.

May I suggest that opening our homes up to guests would also help keep families on their best behavior - *company behavior*! Husbands and wives are less likely to squabble. The children will be more inclined to help clean and look forward to the visiting time. (Just make sure your entire family is home, for safety reasons, and that you do not invite strangers over.)

What if everyone is too busy to visit you? Then consider opening your gates to the *halt*, the *lame*, the *blind*, the *elderly* and the *lonely*. These are the forgotten ones in our communities who would dearly love this kind of human kindness. These are your neighbors and church members who don't get much opportunity for visiting. These are the friends we don't often think of when having a party or get-together.

Mother's Book of Home Economics

You could also make this visiting hour any way you like. It could be a time of having tea, playing board games, gardening parties, or Bible studies. Or just sit and enjoy the conversation with light refreshments, having a break from your normal routine.

In Victorian times, people would have calling cards. When they visited someone who was not home, they would leave their card, so the owner would know they had stopped by. This was before telephones, which are great for verbal visits, but leave out a more personal time of a proper visit.

If "The Visiting Hour" cannot be made a common custom in the U.S., perhaps many of us could start the trend ourselves. Getting the word out with little invitations sent to friends, family, church members and neighbors would be a good start. It would bring a smile, and delight the heart. It would be a lovely form of *hospitality in the home* for this current age.

45

Chore Letters for My Children

This morning, I was feeling overwhelmed. I have been doing a lot of housework. Amy (15) has been ill, so I was doing her chores as well as my own. Then I remembered what I went through a few months ago. I wrote about my homemaking binder and how it solved my problem of delegating housework to the children. At times I can get **selfish** and want to do all the work myself. (It is a sickness - smiles.) But I cannot do everything. Over time, it will wear me out.

So today, I sat down at my dining room table and wrote a letter to each of my children (still at home). Here is what I wrote:

(Age 17) 1. Dear Matthew,

Please clean the game room. Please take all the empty wood pellet bags out of the livingrooom.

Love Mom.

(Age 15) 2. Dear Amy,

Please clean your room. Please bake a cake for Daddy. Please wash the kitchen and bathroom floors.

Love Mom.

(Age 12) 3. Dear John,

Please clean your room. Please clean the bathroom, and take out all the trash.

Love Mom.

These sweet letters were handed to each child. They smiled and cheerfully did their work.

I was delighted.

46

The History of Our Financial Lives

When I was a young teenager, I was intrigued by the cash books in my local store. I bought one and brought it home. From that day forward, I did my best to keep track of my income and spending. I started earning money when I was 11 years old. I did a variety of things like sales, cleaning and babysitting. When I was 15, I had my first real job in a clothing distribution center. I continued to keep track of my spending in my little book, even after I married just a few years later. At that point, I no longer worked. I started to keep a *household* account. Because of this, I can now see my budget from when I had one or two children. I can see what I was buying and how much things cost. It is an amazing history!

Many years later, when my oldest child was around 10 years old, I bought her a cash book. I taught her how to write down her income and expenses. I still have her book and love to read it over. I can sense the excitement in her entries. I enjoyed seeing how she wrote down what she bought, or the income she received. She was thrilled when she would *find* money while cleaning. She would promptly write this down, even if it was 25 cents.

As my children became of age (around 10 years old), I bought each one their own book. They enjoyed writing things down, but as they got older, the practice fell away. I intend to buy each one a new book this coming year and encourage them to keep track of their financial histories.

Right now, I am having trouble finding old fashioned cash books in the local stores. People seem to prefer computer spreadsheets and such. Sadly, my current cash book is more expensive. Even though I'd rather the old cash book of yesteryear, this one does serve its purpose.

It is harder to keep track of all the things I buy. There are just so many needs and expenses. I am looking for ways to cut back. This coming year, I plan to *consume* less. I want to *spend* less. I want the items I *do* buy to be worth writing about.

Mother's Book of Home Economics

47

How Much is a Housewife Worth?

It amazes me that people still think homemakers lay around and do nothing. Obviously it varies in each family, but for the most part, a working- class housewife is very busy, and saves her husband a fortune.

Here are some examples of what she does on a regular daily/ or weekly basis. (Please note - I am speaking generally here. This is just a list of very common examples of what many housewives do at home) -

FOOD

1. Cooks Homemade food (saves money on restaurants).

2. Her home cooking keeps the family more healthy (less doctor bills or health troubles).

3. Her homemade meals and snacks fill the family up, so they are not as likely to eat large amounts of expensive store -bought junk food and snack items.

4. Her meal planning and frugal shopping strategies is like doing inventory-control in a restaurant. She works hard to avoid waste and excessive spending, keeping the grocery budget in line.

TRANSPORTATION

5. If she is home most of the time, she is not wasting money on gas, or impulse spending. There is less wear and tear on the car.

Being home helps her be more creative and resourceful. When she is less stressed, she can do more work at home. (This is not to say she should never go out!)

MAID SERVICE

6. It would cost $40 and up each week to hire a maid to deep clean the house. This includes washing floors, dusting, vacuuming, cleaning bathrooms and scrubbing the kitchen. The housewife does these jobs herself. *She also trains her children to help with these chores.*

CHILD CARE AND EDUCATION

7. Hiring a babysitter or putting the children in day care can cost something like 100 plus dollars each week. A Housewife who is home, can take on this job herself, saving a fortune of the household funds.

8. Tutoring, teaching and training of young children can generally be done by the housewife. Some homeschool their children which saves a fortune in "back-to-school" clothes, tuition, and transportation.

MEDICAL CARE

9. Mothers who are home can nurse their families back to health, and help maintain their well-being. They can also help prevent the spread of germs and build up immune systems with their careful nursing. Mom will certainly bring sick ones to the doctor when necessary, but she is able to generally care for many things on her own.

10. Housewives are also called on for psychology. They listen and guide and help solve the family troubles. Their loving concern and attention soothes the aches of others and helps them back on the right track. Since these mothers are home-focused, they are not being pulled in all directions. They have the time to peacefully handle a crisis when it comes along.

HOUSING

11. She is generally more content with a less expensive home. There is no need to maintain an expensive two-income property. This saves money on insurance, repairs, maintenance, upkeep, mortgages, and so much more.

12. The housewife can do her own frugal decorating. She can keep a nice (yet humble) home with all the time she has at her disposal.

PEACE

13. Have you ever noticed the joy of going into a home where the mom is home and happy? The house looks fairly neat. The children are being cared for. There is good food waiting to be served. It is a happy place to be. [Is there a dollar amount for that?] Of course, this

is not to say that a housewife will never get grumpy. How boring would that be? - gentle smiles.

BIBLE TRAINING

14. The Housewife is able to have time to teach her children the Bible; to read with them and to encourage them to have strong religious values. Abraham Lincoln grew up in a home where the Bible was valued, respected, and read. The Word of the Lord brings wisdom and this helps raise good citizens. When a Home has the constant presence and influence of a godly mother, such great things can happen to a nation! [What is this worth in dollars and cents?]

(Are we, as a nation, losing more than just money when a diligent housewife is no longer at home?)

Please consider adding up how much is spent each month when a housewife *doesn't* do these things at home. I know it would be time consuming, but those dollars and cents add up to a considerable sum of money, which could be used for so many other things. Imagine taking that monthly figure and multiplying it by 12, then multiply that by several years, and you will have an amazing nest egg that will astound you.

What if having mom home made it possible for the family to NEED LESS INCOME? Would the Dads be able to spend more time at home? Would the family have more time together?

Perhaps this is one way of getting off the common money quest, and of hiring out all the work a housewife is capable of doing at home.

Now tell me, how much do you think a housewife is worth? And what other ways is she saving her family a fortune?

48

Spending the Day in the Kitchen

I was very brave today. While Amy (15) was out, I went into her room and gathered up her dishes. I believe they had been there since yesterday (if not longer - horrors!). I soaked them in steaming hot water and dish liquid. They were soon sparkling clean. Then I washed more dishes and scrubbed counters and had a lovely time.

I have the leisure of tending to my home duties and being with my family. *I am truly blessed.*

Later, I turned on some old-time gospel music and sat on a stool near the counter with some hot chocolate. I was close to the stove and the sink - the places I spend most of my time. I looked out at the living room and saw our wood stove and the pretty, snowy view out the front windows. *It is a pleasant place to be.*

I thought I would share my happiness with my boys. I prepared an orange for each one. I peeled and separated the pieces and placed them on decorative tea plates. Then I went into each boy's room and brought their treats.

I was ready to start supper. I made two pans of meatloaf. Those would take an hour and a half to bake. So I tidied some more, then I sat back on my stool. I enjoyed sipping hot chocolate and listening to the pleasant music.

Then I remembered Mr. White. Well, he would certainly like a nice orange too, right? So I prepared one and brought it to him. He gave me a startled look, and said *he felt special*. I realized each one of them thought they were the only one who got an orange. (smiles)

Soon it was time to peel potatoes, make stuffing and get the corn ready. I smiled and enjoyed my kitchen work. *I adored being home and having all the time in the world.* I loved being in my kitchen and taking breaks to do laundry. I wish I had something to iron. I will have to do that this week.

The nicest thing in the world is to clean a kitchen that is not messy. *If one putters around all day long, making things nice and cleaning as one goes along, it makes things very cozy.* (No one enjoys cleaning a messy kitchen or a messy house.) It also makes things very easy to prepare little treats for the family to surprise them.

I want to be remembered for my kitchen work. I want to be the Mother who was always in the kitchen, smiling and making delicious food to comfort the family and brighten the home.

May it be so.

49

The Old Time Family Gathering

"*What shall we do now?*" Here is a question from a parlour guest. They have just had tea, walked about the room, played a little on the piano, and want a new idea for a bit of fun.

Perhaps two are in the corner playing a game of checkers, with deep concentration. Perhaps one of the ladies sits by the fire, busy with some handi-work. Another comes by to see her progress, asking for pointers on her own embroidery project.

Now one offers to read a bit of poetry to the group; Or a bit of Charles Dickens to bring a bit of culture, education and character to the minds of the parlour guests.

Dinner is announced. . . All commence to a formal table for a happy time of dining with one other.

- - - - - -

I wonder if this old time gathering is possible in this day of television, computer, and mass consumer shopping. There are sports programs, and holiday movies to entertain guests. There are computers which call us to visit online. People are planning their financial adventures, and want to shop at all the evening and next day sales. But what if we took a bit of yesteryear and made it possible for our families today? What if we ignored the diversions of our time and really sat around the parlour and passed the time in a lovely, peaceful way. . . *Just for a little while.*

50

30 – Minute Cleaning Marathon

I don't know anyone who enjoys cleaning up a *big mess*. Personally, I like to take my time with housework, to take pride and delight in the process of making a home. However, when the kitchen is a wreck - after a big meal, I need to get things in order quickly. This calls for some marathon cleaning.

This is what I do:

1. Put on my ankle weights and set the timer for 30 minutes. (The weights help me work quickly, like I am doing a workout.)

2. Clean the sink, then fill it with hot water and start soaking dishes. (We don't have a dishwasher.)

3. Clean the counters.

4. Clean the stove.

5. Start washing dishes, drying them and putting them away.

6. I look at the clock and see I have 10 minutes left, this motivates me to work quickly without taking a break.

7. Soak the pans.

8. Sweep the Floor.

9. Wipe down the appliances.

10. Wash the pans.

All finished.

When I do this kind of marathon cleaning, I have much more free time for leisure.

Mother's Book of Home Economics

51

Building a Strong Work Ethic in our Children

Mr. White and I come from blue-collar, working class families in suburban towns south of Boston. We both grew up working around the house, working in the yard, and working in our neighborhoods.

I don't remember my parents giving me spending money. But I always remember working for those extra things I wanted in life. I used to walk at least one mile every day to elementary school, and then later to the bus stop for the higher level schools. When I was in high school, I walked several miles a day (*yes, even in winter*). This was part of the work ethic. This was part of learning not to depend on others for things we should be doing for ourselves. Of course, this was before we feared crime, as this current culture has to worry about. This was when neighbors knew neighbors, knew your parents and watched out for all the kids. This was when communities were stable and safe. It was before broken homes became rampant and people moved in and out of neighborhoods faster than we could get to know them.

There was a tiny store on the corner near our school. Every day, we kids would stop in there to get a drink, an ice cream or a little candy. We would use our own money. This was earned babysitting, doing yard work, and selling papers or magazine subscriptions.

When I got older, I worked at a few companies. This provided me with money for clothes, the movies, or eating at restaurants. All my friends worked for their money too. Even though we lived in a relatively wealthy community, we all had a strong work ethic. Our parents didn't give us our spending money. *We all earned it.*

When I met my husband, at the age of 17, I was working as a secretary in a marine insurance agency, right near the water. It was a lovely place and a great job. Clients would come in to pay their insurance premiums for their yachts. I was surrounded by wealth and privilege but I still worked for what I had, as we all did. None of us thought the rich clients had a free ride. We all knew they worked for what they had.

When I became engaged, I quit my job and started to prepare for a family of my own. Mr. White and I had a contract * and I never had to work (at a job) again. Both of us still worked hard, but in different ways. Me at home, and him at a job. This example to our children was invaluable.

When we started to have children, we taught them the value of money and the value of hard work. They had ways of earning money around the house and helping me with any home-business I had undertaken for their sake. Part of homeschooling, over the years, was learning to be productive, and how to run a business.

Later, we bought a country store. Our children, from as young as 5 years old, worked to help us in our business. They had plenty of opportunities to earn money by working for us.

When the children were very young, I gave them extra work around the house every day. This was optional work and paid anywhere from 5 cents to 25 cents. They thought this was a fortune and eagerly earned their spending money. I still remember the pride Rachel (now 24, but then 5 years old) had when we walked into a little restaurant to pick up our take-out order. She wanted to buy herself a drink and used her own money. She looked at her little sister and said, *"I worked hard for that money!"* I could tell the lessons were sinking in. And while others, at times, would scoff that I required the children to work, they cannot deny that my children all have a strong work ethic. These children are dependable and reliable and put in a good day's work.

This is the *blue -collar working class.* These are the kind of values that made America strong. Sadly, children of today don't understand about delayed gratification. They want everything before they earn the money to buy it. This is dangerous to their own livelihood and for our society. One of the greatest things we mothers can teach our children, is to *wait* and to *work* and to *save*, and then to spend. But never before the money is earned. . . **Never.**

* "Contract" - see page 196.

52

Winter Memories of Struggling to Keep Warm

I remember my father cleaning out the fireplace and crumpling up newspaper to start a warm fire. We would sit in the living room and enjoy the cozy warmth. On other days, Mom would stand in the hall, listening for our heater to click on. Then she would adjust the dial to help keep us warm. Most of the time, we wore sweaters or extra layers of clothing. We have always had to bundle up!

It is always a struggle to keep warm during a New England winter. We have to expect large heating bills. The children must all have thermals, gloves and hats. They need boots and warm sweaters and sweatshirts.

Many families are struggling to pay their bills. A few years ago, when the gas crisis was out of control, heating fuel costs were oppressive! I went to the county fair that summer and picked up a little booklet put out by the government. It was full of sad letters from local Vermont residents who could not afford to keep warm. They were going without food just to buy heat. Some had lost their jobs and were facing homelessness. Others talked about what it was like to freeze in their own homes. It was a devastating book, and it was all true!

The little luxuries in life, become warmth and basic food. There is nothing like walking into a warm house on a freezing day to brighten the spirits! Warmth is the ultimate basic need in the winter.

Have you ever read "The Long Winter" by Laura Ingalls Wilder? I cannot even imagine being that cold! But somehow, that family survived. Somehow, through creativity and hard work, they got through that bitterly cold winter.

One of the most depressing things in this world, is sitting in your own home and being so cold you cannot do basic housework. I've had a few winters like that here, before we had our wood stove put in. I cannot believe what a difference a wood stove makes!

We used to live in an enormous beach house. There were so many rooms! But each one had a set of doors. Even the dining room had 2 sets of doors to close it in and keep it warm. We had to close off portions of the house because we could not keep the entire place heated.

One year, when all my children were little, we lost electricity. We had no heat or fireplace or any way to keep warm. We ended up staying with a relative for a few days until our power was restored. What a blessing to have family who can help in such an important time of need! What a blessing to be warm and surrounded by loved ones who want you cozy and happy!

This winter, I am doing my best to keep the house warm. I am planning to bake fresh warm muffins and breads. I want to make soups and stews and have pleasant things to refresh the souls of my family. It is a ministry just to keep everyone warm and well fed this year!

53

To Use Coupons – Or Not

There is a tremendous focus on coupons right now. If we are not careful, we can end up with a focus on shopping, rather than home-life. A few months ago, I subscribed to emails from "deals" / "couponing" blogs. They certainly know what they are doing, but it made my mind spin. I do not want to think about what I can buy all the time. It was overwhelming for me and I unsubscribed. What I'd like to do today, is offer some kind of balance. Should we use coupons or not? This depends on your circumstances, the kind of life you are living, and your area. I am going to share 4 situations with you. 1. *What my Mother did.* 2. *How I managed to live frugally with 4 children and no coupons.* 3. *My shopping with a heavy coupon focus when I had five small children.* 4. *What I am doing now - in a rural area with little resources, and three teenagers still at home.*

1. **What My Mother did:**

We lived in a lovely, old home in Massachusetts. My mother was an excellent cook. She also had four children who wanted to eat all the time. I often went to the grocery store with her. If I wanted a special treat - such as *poptarts* or some *sugary cereal* - Mom would have me use my own money. She rarely bought those items. I remember coming home from school and looking around. I always thought there was nothing to eat. Why? Because there were no frozen pizzas or canned chef boyardee! Yet, when meal-time came, Mom made delicious food that would fill us up - it was always homemade. We would have things like chicken with potatoes, assorted vegetables and bread. Mom rarely ever bought convenience food and I never saw her use coupons. Do you know why Mom didn't want convenience food? Because if she bought a couple of frozen pizzas, they were gone in a matter of minutes and we children were *still hungry*. Those were the days when we were not allowed to "spoil our dinner!" . . The good old days!

One time, I spent the night at a friend's house. I was offered ice cream. We looked in the freezer and saw 3 different kinds. I could not even imagine what that was like! If Mom bought ice cream - she only bought one kind and it was only for a special occasion. Desserts were reserved for weekends, holidays or other special occasions. This was also the way my mother was raised. Grandma made homemade foods, with little meat. They had a special cake or other treat on Sundays. If you wanted a drink or snack - well, there was always water, carrots or apples. You know what? We always had food. We never went hungry. And we had a lovely, happy home.

My Mother's way is what I call "traditional home economics." It is the ideal, in my opinion.

2. **How I managed to live frugally with 4 children and no coupons.**

When my fourth baby was born, my husband and I lived in a large house with a beautiful kitchen. It was a temporary, winter rental near the ocean. I fell in love with the kitchen the moment we walked in the door. I had plenty of counter space, a dishwasher and a wonderful stove. We were living frugally and saving up to buy a house. During this time, I bought an amazing book. It was called The "Tightwad Gazette II," by Amy Dacyczyn (I later bought her Complete book containing all three volumes.) In this book, she talked about why she never used coupons, and how to economically stock your pantry with the basics. She also described why menu plans don't always work. In her experience, as long as you had a full pantry of everything you needed, you could make just about anything without having to run to the market for extra ingredients. Her ideas were wonderful. I started buying cheaper versions of flour and other foods to make my homemade meals more economical. I learned to make simpler meals. For example - you can use a plain tomato sauce for homemade pizza. It tastes fine even if it is a bulk-can of a generic version. I was making tortellini, pizza, bread, muffins, Italian bread and more - all from scratch and only spending a very small amount of money. I was thrilled. Amy also explained how name brand cereal and other convenience foods that we normally use coupons to buy, don't fill us up! If a child had a homemade banana muffin for breakfast, he is less likely to be hungry again 20 minutes later. In other words - homemade foods are more economical because the children need *less food* to fill them up. When they are eating those coupon-purchased meals or snacks, they need more and more to finally be hungry. During this time of my life, with the four small children, I successfully used her ideas and we lived well on a small income, without the use of coupons. We were happy. My heart and mind were home-centered, rather than

Mother's Book of Home Economics

shopping-centered. I didn't have to waste time cutting coupons or feeling obsessed by sales or savings. It was a lovely time of life.

3. My shopping with a heavy coupon focus when I had five small children.

Shortly after my fifth child was born, I came across a new book. It was "Shop, Save, and Share," by Ellie Kay. This was amazing! Not only did I learn her tricks for shopping with coupons, I also learned how to buy things for those in need using unwanted coupons. I was thrilled. This was fun! Every Sunday, I bought one or two newspapers and planned my attack. I spent 30 - 40 minutes with one of my daughters, poring over the sales ads and matching up the coupons. We made a budget, menu plan and shopping list. The children and I would then head out to three supermarkets and buy all the "deals" and also use our coupons. We had plenty of food and enjoyed this "game." However, in hindsight, I realize that we spent more money during that time period (a few years) than any other time in my marriage. I do not regret this, because at that time, I was very ill with cancer and I really couldn't do a lot, myself, to manage our kitchen. My oldest daughter (from the age of 9 to 15) learned to run a home and bake and cook and became very skilled. Another serious problem that came up during this time, was that I had a major shopping focus. We spent far too much money in other areas as well- including toys, clothes, recreational items, etc. I was always interested in going somewhere, or finding the next sale. I did not feel settled or home-centered. I share this only to show a different perspective, not to say that coupons are wrong. But to share what I experienced in order to help you make your own decision.

4. What I am doing now - in a rural area with little resources, and three teenagers still at home.

Our family moved to Vermont several years ago. In this area, there are no malls. There is no Wal-Mart. There are very few places to shop. It was major culture shock for me and took me a long time to stop *wanting* to go shopping. I remember, after living here for a year, finally taking a "road trip" to the nearest Wal-Mart in New Hampshire. All I wanted to do was go back home, to my small, rural community and get away from the crowds and the shopping-mindset. I was settled. I was home-centered, and I loved it.

Currently, I rarely ever use coupons. For the past four weeks, our local supermarket gave out $10 off coupons if we spent $100. I used it for three of those weeks but found it difficult. I never spend $100 in just one store. I didn't like it. I didn't want to *buy* things just to get that discount.

As for my current shopping plan, it has evolved into something quite interesting. When we first moved here, we bought a country store. We had to stock inventory and always have merchandise available for the customers. We had a list of everything we sold and I checked the distributor order forms and local sales flyers to see what we wanted to buy. I was often able to buy things at a drastically reduced price, by going to a local store and bringing that merchandise to our own customers. For example - the Pepsi company charged us $1.69 for a 2-liter of soda. They expected us to sell this for $1.99. Outrageous, right? So when Pepsi went on sale for 89 cents a bottle, I would buy 40 or 50 bottles (as long as the store had no limit) and bring them into our business to sell to our customers at a much more reasonable price. The clerks and managers at the supermarket knew I was doing this and were so helpful. Because of this, I was able to buy all kinds of food items our customers wanted and charge a fair price. They saved money because it saved them the trip of driving all the way into town. Everyone was happy.

How does this relate to my own home? We sold that store 3 years ago. But I am still using the inventory principle for my own pantry. I combined Amy's ideas (from the Tightwad Gazette) with our store idea to make sure we always have food.

First let me say this- we have experienced times of wealth and times of poverty in our marriage. During the poverty phases, we learned to enjoy simpler foods and let go of many name-brand items. My husband used to want Miracle Whip and Maxwell house. Nothing else would ever be good enough. But after some bouts with poverty, he learned to enjoy generic versions. This is important. Most people are not willing to do this. But take whatever, of the following ideas, that will work for you.

1. I buy 2 or 3 bottles of generic mayonnaise, ketchup and mustard.

2. I keep 2 bags of granulated sugar at home at all times. (We go through this very quickly.) I use the store brand version.

3. I buy a large can of generic coffee. If the name brand is on sale and costs less than generic, I buy that instead.

Mother's Book of Home Economics

- (This is serious... If I have a well-stocked pantry, then I have a home-mindset, rather than a shopping mind-set. I will not need to run to the store every couple of days because I run out of the basics. I keep *more than one* on my shelves at all times.)

4. For meat - I will buy 10 packages or more of ground turkey, chicken or burger when they are marked down. For example- yesterday, Purdue ground turkey was on sale for $2.99 a pound. It was marked down by $2 because it needed to be sold quickly. I got it for 99 cents. (Now I realize people can buy meat more frugally than this, but I am not the kind of girl who likes to work with whole chickens, turkey or other such animals. I want the butcher to grind it up so I don't have to see any of what it looked like before!) Personally, I don't eat meat at all. But the rest of my family does. We combine one of these packages with pasta, potatoes, etc. to make a large, filling meal. So If I paid 99 cents for the meat, $1 for the pasta, another $1 for a little cheese and corn, this kind of meal only costs $2.99 and feeds a hungry family.

5. I can buy a 12- box package of store brand macaroni and cheese on sale for $5 or... I can buy 5 boxes of Prince pasta for $5 and make them go much further.

6. We can make homemade pizza with flour, oil, salt, and seasonings - without expensive yeast, and feed a hungry family for very little money.

7. Recently, store brand mozzarella cheese was on sale. But they were out- of- stock! I looked around and realized I could buy a much

Mother's Book of Home Economics

larger bag for less than the sale prize. I came home with a large, bulk- bag of cheese, so the children had plenty of pizzas that week!

8. We have a dollar store here. That's where I buy trash bags, paper towels and dish liquid. (We don't have a dishwasher.)

9. There is a small, charming village market nearby. It is probably 800 square feet but it is packed with wonderful, economical merchandise. Every week, I buy my milk, butter, eggs, bread, cheese, etc. from them. Their regular prices are cheaper than my supermarket sale prices. (Some people might visit outlet stores for cheap bread, or discount stores. It all depends on what is in your own area.)

10. If I can find beef and potatoes on sale, I will make a large pot of beef stew. I also share this with my parents (who live with us- in an in-law apartment on the first floor of our house.) Beef stew is expensive, but I can make it with only 3 ingredients - potatoes, beef and carrots. I also add seasoning. This might cost me $6 and will feed my parents, my husband, and three of my children. I also make buttermilk biscuits to help fill everyone up. It is important to have some bread, crackers, or side dish to round out an expensive main dish.

Frankly, you can starve to death on processed, junk foods. It is so important to learn how to prepare hearty, inexpensive, homemade foods for your family. I realize we love our name brands. Personally, I won't eat generic pasta. I can't stand the taste of it. We don't have to be food martyrs. But we should try to find some balance. It is a wonderful treat to have a little Kraft Macaroni and Cheese, or Ellios

Pizza. We should still enjoy these goods, but not necessarily on a regular basis because they are very expensive in the long run. I am more likely to buy name-brand processed foods when I am very ill and can't manage my kitchen. But the ideal, *the rule*, for me, is to make it myself.

To use coupons or not. . That is a great question. It is a personal decision. Do whatever you find best in your own situation.

My final thoughts- do I use coupons? Certainly! But not every week. I am not seeking them out. I am not printing them off the internet and I am not buying the weekly newspaper to find coupons. But I do use them on occasion as needed.

What about you? Do you have a shopping mind-set or a home-mind-set? Is it possible to find a balance between using coupons and not using them?

54

What I Learned from My Husband's Weariness

My husband comes home from work with a hurting back and is exhausted. He slowly walks to his room, looking almost hunched over and defeated. Despite his physical suffering, this man will still help the children fix things, or talk with them. He will still fix the car or carry in 40 pound bags of wood pellets. He does not sit in a chair and boss our children around, even though he has every right to ask them for help. When they see him working so hard without complaint, their admiration for him, their love and respect soars!

He patiently deals with their moods and *they listen to him*, when he asks for quiet. I have never seen him argue with them when they are being rude. He does not try to tell them to "respect him," or say "You will not talk to me like that." He simply says "enough," and goes about his day. The children's normal murmurings fade out and they are calm again.

I have seen him work harder than I could ever imagine myself working. Yet, he does it in a sacrificial way. He wants nothing in return. He works for our food, our home and little presents here and there to cheer us all up. I have seen this man go without new shoes or clothes just so we could have something we need or want.

When I look into the eyes of this weary man, I am inspired to work harder at home. I want to have that same sacrificial love for my family and home. I want to give up more and more of my little selfishness. While he never says much to teach us how to do this - his work ethic, his tremendous love for us, his never complaining, the children and I are constantly learning from him.

55

Not Happily Married

I no longer use the word "*happily*" when describing my marriage. Does this mean I am not happy? Of course not! I am delighted and grateful to have Mr. White for my husband. We have been married for almost a quarter of a century. But for me to say I am "happily married" implies that we live in a fairy tale world. Those words may very well discourage someone else. Why? Because marriage is not really about happiness.

Mr. White and I have stood together and faced suffering, trials, tears, discouragement and tragedy. We have been pruned and given up more and more of 'self' for the good of our family. How can this be called "*happy?*"

Marriage is more about commitment and creating a lifelong family unit. It is being together through all of life's difficulties.

Yet there is a somber joy. . a contentment. . . a feeling of unbelievable gratefulness and humbleness in a long marriage. We are co-laborers in our home and life.

So for me to say we are "happily married" is superficial. It doesn't share the truth of the matter. And that is that we are *gratefully* married and have tremendous love and respect for each other. We do this through tears and laughter.

The marriage story, *the secret of a good marriage*, is the sadness in one's eyes from the pain of life, but the deep reverence the couple has for each other. Perhaps to say we are "gratefully married" or that we are "blessed to be married" is more accurate.

But the greatest description of all, is the comfort of knowing we will stand ***side-by-side***, through every hardship, through every joy, and despite any pain. . . . for as long as we both shall live.

Mother's Book of Home Economics

56

Do Not Disturb

At any moment, we are troubled by many things. Our peace, in this world, is always on the brink of danger. A feeling of calmness, *that things are okay*, is often elusive.

The main offense, that robs us of our peace, are the words of others. This may be news, gossip, slander, troubles, or facts. When someone speaks words of discord to us, or speaks words of facts that will upset us, they have spoken something dangerous that will disturb our souls.

Everything we see, or hear, or experience, does not have to be shared with others. What we say to others, can cause them harm, even if the information is true. What we share with others, even in confidence, can cause them pain, even if that was not the intention. Do not trouble the mind of others. Do not disturb their peace.

The Chofetz Chaim tells us that *"Loshan hora (lit., evil talk) is defined as information which is either derogatory or **potentially harmful** to another individual.. . . . A statement that could potentially bring harm to someone - be it financial, physical, psychological or otherwise - is loshon hora, even if the information is not negative."*

I cannot even count the number of times someone told me something, or shared some news with me, that I considered to be gossip. They considered it to be telling me something important or what I needed to know, but I considered it a disturbing of my peace. Often, people tell me things just before I face a trial. Or just before I am about to go to sleep. Then I am troubled for hours. But I keep the "news" to myself, so as not to spread the harm of a disturbed mind.

Will there ever come a day when genuine gossip will cease? *Genuine* gossip is sharing truth with others. Even this is a vexation of spirit. Why bring people down with facts and news and sad things?

When will we learn to speak life into others? When will we learn to share positive, uplifting words that will encourage a weary soul?

Be quiet. . . Be meek. . . **Keep it to yourself.** . . It is a blessing, *a good deed*, to spare someone the pain of negative talk. More often than not, *they really don't need to know* what you are about to say.

57

Tending the Home

There are many distractions, in life, which keep us from housework and a calm focus on home. These distractions can include anything from clutter and disorganization, to excessive busyness or a gluttony of television.

A list of daily chores for housekeeping is helpful for staying on track. We also gain a wonderful sense of peace when we polish furniture, sweep floors and iron the linens. These tasks show our love for home, if done with a right heart.

They say there is a secret ingredient in good recipes. This ingredient is what makes the food amazing and delicious. That same secret ingredient is needed for a well-kept home. It is "love." When we put love in our work, it gives us a rising sense of honor. We will go the farthest mile, despite weariness, for the love of what we are doing.

When we care for the home, by our daily work, and with a right heart, we create an amazing retreat for those around us. But truly, we are the ones who benefit the most, because we will reap the greatest sense of peace and fulfillment.

If we truly realized the greatness of an eternal perspective, and cared for the home out of a sense of devotion for The Master, our will would be so strong that nothing could distract us from so great a task as tending the home.

"Our fair morning is at hand, the daystar is near the rising, and we are not many miles from home. What matter then, of ill-entertainment in the smoky inns of this worthless world? We are not to stay here, and we shall be dearly welcome to Him whom we are going." - Samuel Rutherford, 1600's

58

Importance of Home Economics Training

Keeping the home is a challenging career in itself. We are not unemployed, living in leisure. We have daily work that keeps us busy. It is important that we are trained in the scientific arts of home economics. Here are just some of the things we need to do:

1. Operate and maintain appliances. We also need to understand how new models work and see if they will make our homes more efficient - both in saving labor and money.

2. We need to learn nutrition. This is for the health of our families. This includes our choices in the grocery store, our meal planning, our baking and cooking. We must have basic cooking and shopping skills.

3. Basic Medical Care. We are lay-nurses. We must know how to handle colds, fevers, and minor injuries.

4. Child Care and Development. We need to know the basics of caring for a baby, toddler, child, teenager and young adult.

5. Basic Sewing. We need to be able to, at the very least, repair clothes and sew on buttons. Making clothes for the family, or sewing drapes, and doing embroidery work, etc. are nice, but not essential in today's homes.

6. Laundry and Cleaning. To run a sanitary, efficient home, we must learn the basics of laundry and how to clean a house.

What if you don't know any of this stuff and are struggling at home?

In the early part of the 1900's, homemakers clubs were available in many towns throughout the United States. This was where the women would get together to learn from one another. In my local town's Historical Society, there is a photograph of a group of mothers in a homemaker's club in the 1930's. Their support of one another was wonderful!

Today, we can join quilting clubs, cooking clubs and the like. We can also read books, watch videos and learn in many different ways. The important thing to remember is that we must always continue to sharpen our skills and learn because changes in modern culture and technology affect our work at home.

59

Family Economy

I have been spending a lot of money lately. Each day, it seems, I smile to my husband and say, *"Honey, I am broke."* He then gives me a little extra cash to get through the day. I had been so careful for so long, but many things have come up to cause money to disappear. Either someone has a birthday, event, or a need for special clothes. Or there are extra expenses. *Or maybe I forgot how to be creative?*

I was thinking about hard working Immigrant families from the early 1900's. Almost everyone in the family worked together (often at home) to earn enough cash to feed, house and clothe each other. Money was not something to be squandered! What I would like to do today is consider how they would handle special events where gifts were required.

- If someone needed special clothes for a church event, wedding, or graduation. I am sure the pride of that family would kick in and *all* would work extra hard to earn enough to buy the clothes. Contrast this with today's thinking. We would spend our bill money, savings, or *charge* the clothes, rather than find ways to earn all that extra money.

- If there was a birthday, they would not go to the local mall to buy all kinds of presents for each other. I am not sure what they would do, but I can guess they would make something, or pitch in together to buy one thing that was greatly wanted or needed. Gifts were also much more rare than they are today, making them far more appreciated.

It also seems to me that money was earned for more basic purposes in the old days. I don't understand why, even in my own mind, I have to fight against the constant *supposed* need for money that I tend to use *and waste* for my own convenience.

One of the greatest things we can do as a family, is to work together to keep expenses down. We can work together (with our own hands and talents) to cook and to bake and to create, to bless each other.

In this rough economy, how can any of us dare to be frivolous? Sadly, I don't think I will ever shake this constant fight against wasting something so essential to basic living.

60

How the Old Time Mothers Survived Poverty

There are so many families struggling right now. There is never enough food for even the basics of life. Housewives need encouragement, inspiration and ideas in order to survive on very little.

During the War in the 1940's, Britain's government provided citizens with books to help them obtain skills to manage on very little. These were called: "Wartime cookery" and "Make do and Mend." I understand some of these have been recently re-published.

The other day, I cut out material to make two aprons. While I was ironing all the material I was thinking about the depression-era mothers. They would take scraps of fabric and piece them together for quilts. Or they would make rag-rugs. These women were productive, hardworking and creative. They could take the smallest amount of leftovers, from supper, and come up with something amazing the next day.

With knowledge, ideas and inspiration, these women survived poverty. Currently, in America, we are told, by the government, that (in 2009) a family of 5, earning less than $25,790 is living in poverty. It does not take much to be poor in this current age.

Housing costs are high, utility bills are outrageous and food costs are rising. Here are some things the Old time mothers did:

1. Water down the milk.

2. If children were allowed to have a soda, they had to share it.

3. If, during a holiday, the family had soda, they would fill the cups with ice and add a little water before pouring the soda. The children never knew what "real" or "straight" soda tasted like until they were grown.

4. Cut up one apple or orange and divide between everyone in the family. Serve on their lunch or supper plate.

5. Sew and mend rips in the clothes. (Are we doing this today?)

6. Make a big pot of soup, then do the housework and laundry. The soup cooks all day - it is an inexpensive meal and goes far. Just serve it with muffins or biscuits.

7. Bake something every other day - muffins, bread, biscuits. Leave this out, wrapped up, on the table or counter. It will help fill everyone up and keep them from snacking on junk or feeling hungry (deprived).

8. When there is nothing to drink, Mother would make tea. Those tea bags were re-used all day long to fill cup after cup. Mother served tea on tea plates and kept the tea bags on those little plates for re-use later in the day.

9. Mother saved jars (we can save spaghetti-sauce jars today) and kept them clean, storing them in the cabinet. When the family would go out, she would fill that jar with cold water so everyone would have something to drink.

As I was doing some hand-sewing yesterday, I thought how important it was to keep busy. I prayed as I sewed. I was keeping busy with the home arts and this soothed my soul. If we mothers of today, could just work hard around our homes, and pray for courage, we could make it on very little. We would also start believing more in miracles and trust God so much more than we do now. So many blessings come to the diligent, brave housewives. May we all be found worthy.

61

Rural Homemaking

Yesterday, I tried to go out on an errand. I had my grandbaby with me. We were to do the grocery shopping for the Estate. We drove down the long driveway, then two houses down before the car *died*. I pulled into the neighbor's driveway, took baby out of the car, and walked home.

I am home-bound in a rural area. I no longer have a running vehicle for my own personal use. Yet, I am okay and at peace with my circumstances.

I will bake and cook more. . . I will clean more. . . I will sew and knit and read. . . I will decorate and rearrange rooms to make them more pleasant. This large old house can always use some extra attention. I will make the downstairs rooms more *guest-ready*. I will spend more time enjoying the grounds, and my humble gardens.

Rural Homemaking is nothing new. Cars were not even commonly used until the early 1900's. People stayed home more, and used horses to get around. I remember reading this book by a "Yankee" Vermonter about his growing up years. * There was so much common sense wisdom in his experiences. Adults would scold people who wanted to go out all the time, by saying things like *"better off staying t' home where [you] b'longed, and shouldn't ought* *to go gallivanting all over Creation."* He also described how his Mother (and most other women of the time) did not feel comfortable leaving home in a car. She wouldn't even go for a drive until she was sure her house was clean from top to bottom just in case she got killed. She would say, "I don't want someone else to have to clean up the place for a funeral." His Mother made sure all the children were freshly washed and wearing clean clothes if they even went to the store. It was an ordeal, which tells us that going out was not a common, daily event.

My mother-in-law spent most of her time at home. She had visitors, mostly her grown children and grandchildren. She was a loving hostess, and life-long homemaker. She had little flower gardens, and enjoyed doing projects like painting an old chair. Pretty birds frequented her Massachusetts yard. She did all her laundry in the walk-out basement, and hung the clothes on rows of clothesline that Papa set up for her near the washer. She loved home, and we always knew where to find her.

In rural areas, without public transportation, or the ability to walk to necessary stores, it is a little more difficult to go without a vehicle. But we will get by. We will make do. It will be my latest challenge, my latest adventure.

Somehow, the needed shopping and errands will be accomplished even if I am completely ensconced at our lovely old home.

* *"Fetched Up Yankee" by Lewis Hill.*

62

The Weary Housewife

I think we all have these ideals of being a good housekeeper. We have set chores, like washing floors, dusting and polishing on a regular basis. One day last week, I enjoyed an entire day of just cleaning. The house looked lovely. I took short breaks as needed, and paced myself accordingly to avoid becoming tired. I was able to work in the kitchen and cook nice meals. It was the perfect housekeeping day.

But sometimes the "ideal" housewife is impossible. We are a culture of exhausted mothers. We have sicknesses, and distractions that are making it harder and harder for us to enjoy our work in the home. Being our "own" boss would imply that we could stop all unhealthy activities and interferences so we could focus entirely on mothering, homemaking and being a good wife. But few of us have such courage. Or is it something we have to continually strive for?

The last few days have been miserable for me. I am unbearably weary from health difficulties. I decided, late yesterday afternoon, to put myself on bed - rest for a few days. It's not that I even do too much around the home, it is that my health has been declining for such a long time, there is little I can do anymore. More rest requires me to stop what I love to do. I love and adore keeping house. I love vacuuming and washing floors and cooking meals. It is what I delight in. But my health will not allow it. So back to bed I must go, for a time of respite. Then I will emerge ready to keep house, but at a slower and slower pace.

Yet, I will never give up. . . I will certainly take times of rest and recovery. But I will never stop trying to keep this house for my precious family. We housewives will get knocked down by many things in this life. We must always get up and keep at it. Rest, yes, but keep going. Heaven is waiting at the end, and the eternal rest will be glorious!

63

Comforts of the Old Estate

Old, quaint homes create a sort of ambiance that makes one cheerful. One can even be imaginative and creative with one's life. These types of homes are ideal for artists and inventors.

In our old 1800's house, there is a large, sunny room on the first floor. It is warm and cozy. I can read on the little *Ethan Allen* sofa that we bought at an auction, on the grounds of the home we now own. I can see the front property and enjoy the quiet seclusion of our "estate."

The reality of living in an old house, *when one is of limited means*, is suffering with cold and dreary rooms. Any of us could give in to our difficult circumstances and dwell on that which is unpleasant. We could certainly allow ourselves a few hours, or days, of indulging in melancholy moods, but then to emerge from that with a new zeal and excitement for the *possibilities* can make things so much better.

Does it matter that my *Ethan Allen* couch is designed with an odd color, or that it is ripped up and overly worn from age? *Only to onlookers*. To me it is very comfortable. We keep it covered with a flowery bedspread, and a few throw pillows. As long as the surroundings are neat and tidy, the couch adds a pleasant coziness to the room.

The Homemaker who calls her home an "estate," "cottage," or other such charming term, will find happiness in her daily tasks - making the home pleasant, because she has found a way to make the most of her circumstances. She will not get caught up in the crankiness of family members. She will not get caught up in the neighbor's gossip. She can be a bright light and a joy to those around her because she is dedicated to the ART of creating a comfortable, pretty home - *with what she has*. This becomes her hobby, her vocation, her calling.

I'll admit it is easier to have an "estate" when one has an old house. But a beach house, an apartment, or a mobile home can inspire the residents to bring joy to their guests if the homemaker takes a little time to invent her own little retreat. What would one call an apartment? How about a "flat" (a London term), or think of the charming little places in Italy? What about a mobile home? Could one call it a cabin? Or a camper in the park? There are so many different types of places to live! We just have to find a way to make them special and pleasant. This will bring us comfort. This will bring our family comfort. This is what will motivate and inspire us to keep house, especially on those difficult days.

Mother's Book of Home Economics

64

Ten Children and Housekeeping

I happen to love cleaning and polishing my house. It makes me happy to tidy and make a home. However, this can be hard when there is a large family and babies around. We will have our bad days, when there is a crisis or children are sick, but I want to share with you some ideas to make housekeeping a pleasant experience.

First I will tell you what we did when I had *ten children* here at home. Then I will explain how we managed with *five children* ages 9 and under. Last, I will tell you how I did my housework when I had only *three children* under the age of 5. Hopefully, you will glean some ideas, or inspiration, for your own situation.

Cleaning the House with Ten Children at Home.

When my oldest was 16 years old, I had a small daycare in my house. (My own children, at the time, were ages - 16, 15, 12, 10, and 8.) We took care of five children. It was quite a unique situation and I will explain this. At that time, we owned a store. Three of my oldest children worked there most of the time, along with my husband. Right in the middle of this, I was helping my husband with things like daily operations, inventory, paperwork, and bookkeeping. It took much of my time. However, I was also in the middle of homeschooling 4 of my 5 children. My oldest had just graduated so she was working more in our store. Now here is the question of the day... why did I decide to open a daycare? I missed having babies around! I wanted to be HOME and I love children. So we opened our doors to five children. We had 3 preschoolers, ages 3, 3 and 4. We also had two sweet little babies. One was 4 months old and the other was 6 months old. They were treasures!

Now I must tell you, it is far easier to clean and cook and enjoy home when you have lots of children! This is the best part of family life. There are plenty of helpers, friends, entertainers, etc. There will always be someone there to do the dishes, or hold the baby, or make the toddler laugh. There is always someone there to referee an argument, or teach someone to tie a shoe. There is a lot of laughter and happiness. This was a fun time for me to clean house. Here are some specifics:

1. I only had 2 children (ages 10 and 8) to help with chores during this time, since my oldest three were in- and- out all day, helping my husband with our store.

2. Amy (then 10 years old) and I would take turns holding the babies. We would each have a bottle and feed "our" baby. Then we would switch off to get each one to burp. We had so much fun with those little treasures! Amy learned a lot about raising children and caring for babies. It was on- the- job training and it was fun!

3. In the morning, I would clean the kitchen, do dishes and make breakfast. During this time, one of the older children played with the babies or read to the children.

4. Amy made and served the lunch, while I cared for the children. John (then 8) cleaned up the mess. After everyone ate, it was time for naps, so I would feed and rock one of the babies and put him down to sleep. Once he was settled, I would get the other baby from one of the older children and get that one settled for a nap.

5. In the afternoon, when all the children were up and playing, I vacuumed. They all LOVED to see the vacuum cleaner. They would laugh, sitting on the couch or chairs and just watch.

6. The children were taught to do clean-ups throughout the day. If we were getting ready for story time, we did "10 minute cleanings." Or if we were going outside, we had to hurry and tidy. Having something special planned made it easy for the children to work quickly. They were also very proud of themselves when I inspected their work.

7. We would often have the children busy polishing the chairs, picking up messes or wiping the table. We even invented cleaning jobs just to keep them busy and productive while we did our housework. They felt like they were "helping" us and it was clean up time for everyone.

8. The children only played in specific rooms, so most of the house stayed fairly neat. It is very easy to only have to worry about keeping a couple of rooms clean: kitchen, bathroom, play room – rather than the whole house.

9. I did laundry throughout the day. These were timed around naps so the noise from the dryer didn't interfere with sleeping children.

10. I packed away most of the toys and brought out a basket of "new" ones each day. This created excitement in the children and also made less of a cluttered mess.

11. I have to tell you that we did our best to keep the children reasonably quiet throughout the day. I taught them to have indoor voices. I was very consistent with this. If the children are not running around acting up, yelling, etc., Mom is going to be much more peaceful. But the most important motivator of keeping all those children quiet was because my dear husband slept from 11 am until 6 pm! He worked an early morning shift at our store, and then the late night shift, so he slept during the day. The children could run in our fenced- in play yard and laugh and giggle and yell all they wanted when we were outside. By the time we came back in, they were happy to be quiet for snacks, lunch, stories, or naps.

12. Of course, we had more difficult days when a baby was fussy or sick and I couldn't do much housework. I would depend on the older children to take over. Those were special days, sitting and rocking a baby and just being peaceful.

Five Children under Nine

When my oldest was 9 years old, I had cancer and a newborn baby. I made a chore chart so all the children could do the daily tasks. We even made this fun by giving each child a title position in the house. Someone was "The Chore police." Another child was "The Breakfast Hostess." Someone was in charge of monitoring the use of utilities - "The Electricity Inspector." Each day they had to do laundry, make meals, clean the rooms and sweep. I was very ill and caring for a baby. I could not help them much at all! I spent most of my time on the couch or resting in bed. I helped when I could, but mostly I managed with lists, and praise, and giving out directions.

One of the most helpful things during this time was the fact that we kept the toys in the living room and out of the bedrooms. It made it easier for me to monitor the cleaning.

Cleaning with Three children 5 and under

I had a five year old girl and a four year old girl who were best friends. There really wasn't much to do to keep up with them. We had our daily tasks - meals, snacks, playing, reading, walks, etc. We had a nice routine. I also had a 1 year old baby boy who was such fun for us all. The girls loved to play with him! I did most of the housework alone. I also did all the cooking. I kept the living area nice and neat. Since we didn't have that many children, I had them keep their toys in their bedrooms. That is where they played. So the main part of the house was always clean. Sure, they were allowed to bring in a toy or two, but then had to put it away. They were required to clean up after themselves. We lived a quiet life and stayed home most of the time. This brought us all peace and made it very easy to keep house.

Conclusion

Children who are raised in a home where *everyone* pitches in to clean are more likely to keep their own homes clean. It becomes a habit. It is not enough for them to just clean their rooms or just do the laundry. It is better if they are part of the cooking crew, the kitchen clean up, the vacuuming; decorating, organizing and all the other tasks that help make a home. If Mom is right there loving this part of her life, and is willing to share it with her children, it makes it all worthwhile.

Whether you have *one* child or *ten*, it will take planning to keep things going. Nothing is ever going to be finished. There will always be another mess to clean. The goal is not to have a spotless house at all times, but to enjoy the ongoing process of housekeeping.

65

How to Teach a 2 – Year old to Clean

Many years ago, when my children were small, I was very ill. I had just given birth to my fifth child. The oldest was nine years old. I was being treated for cancer and couldn't do much. I had already taught my children to clean and do most of the housework.

Matthew was 4 years old at that time. He was in charge of our living room. This was where all the children played. We had two large toy boxes in there. Matthew had to pick up all those toys and keep the room neat. Well, one day, he asked me why he had to always clean that room. . . He was such a cutie. . . So I said, "Well, if you don't want to clean, then teach Amy how to do it and then you'll never have to clean it again!"

Amy was 2 years old then. She was an adorable little wild girl. She LOVED her brother so much and was his very best friend. So Matthew sat there on the coffee table and told her what to do. He made the whole thing into this fun game for her. He would say things like, "run and get that bear... now throw it in the toy box...now grab that block and throw it in there too!" He had her racing around the room, laughing and working. She had that room clean in no time. I just stood in the doorway and watched.

When the room was all clean, Matthew crossed his arms over his chest and smiled proudly. He looked back and grinned at me. He never had to clean that room again.

66

The Good Wife

In the old days, Mothers used to hold a special place in the home for Fathers. The children were taught not to sit in his chair. They were taught to serve him first. They were taught to respect their Father as the head of the home.

But somewhere along the way, Mothers became more independent. No longer would they be like Edith Bunker, who did everything for her husband, during the height of the women's lib movement.

I like to think I take good care of Mr. White. I like to think I am a good wife. But yesterday I noticed something had been forgotten. I noticed him on edge and unhappy. I realized it was *my fault*.

I had been talking too much about the children's problems. I had been discussing money and bills. While these conversations have their place, it should not be the all-consuming - day-in-day-out focus of our home life.

When I realized this was happening, I remembered the old farm wives who used to make large meals and feed their weary husbands. They worked tirelessly for the comfort of their men - the providers.

I remembered sweet women, who were wives of great ministers - like Mrs. John R. Rice. I thought of her favorite book, which I have read numerous times. It was something she kept by her bedside and loved dearly. It was called, "God's Ideal Woman," and was written in 1941. Mrs. Rice wrote the foreword for this book. Then I thought of another amazing book, from the same publisher, called, "Beautiful for Thee." This one was published in the 1970's. Ladies, these kinds of books were written before Women's Lib changed a culture. These old books teach us how to be good wives and mothers.

As I thought about these books, I knew what I had to do to cheer up my husband. I asked him if he was comfortable and I resolved to **be silent**. . .

I would be meek and submissive and concern myself only with *the moment,* and Mr. White's happiness here at home. This must be a place of refuge for him. It must be a place of peace and rest. So I went into the kitchen and made a delicious supper. Then we both sat together and quietly read the newspaper. I kept all my opinions and thoughts to myself. I had to learn the art of silence. I had to learn that my husband needed quiet so he could recover from his own worries.

I think Mrs. Bunker had it right all along. She wanted to make sure Archie had his meals and his coffee and his special chair. She created a home for him, a place he wanted to be, despite the feministic pull of the world. She created a place where she served him with love and devotion, and did her very best not to cause him any additional worries.

67

When We Can't Endure a Little Hardship

Living in an old house makes me think about all the struggles the early Americans went through. I visited Plimouth Plantation, in Massachusetts, many times. The tiny little houses the Pilgrims lived in were cold, plain and uncomfortable. The people worked tremendously hard just to survive. *This is hardship.*

In our 1800's house, there are drafts, broken faucets, and plumbing problems. We are always repairing something or trying to make things last. We are also constantly seeking ways to economize. During a recent warm spell, we didn't use our wood pellet stove. Some mornings I was cold, but I just had to wait a few hours for the temperature to rise, and the house would have been heated by the warmth of the sun. It is in our nature to seek ease, comfort and self-indulgence. We have an anti-hardship nature. This is why we waste money, and act spoiled. It came from generations of Americans who forgot what it was like for the Pilgrims and the Pioneers. We are living on *the ease* and "wealth" created by our ancestors. Instead of continuing their traditions, we are sitting back and living like the rich.

In the old days, *struggle* built character. And a little suffering made us grateful.

Now things seem to be handed to us. We lost our ability to endure the rough times. We lost our creativity and ingenuity.

This morning I was thinking about how easy things are for me. I have plenty of free time, and set my own plans for each day. I have good things to eat. I have a lovely home (as long as I work hard to keep it neat). Even though I have so many things to be thankful for, I still grumble and complain when I have to suffer. We modern day Americans come from tough Pioneer stock. But we have weakened and softened over the years. One of the greatest accomplishments would be for us to endure the hard times and learn to sacrifice for the good of our characters.

No one wants to suffer, of course. But if we can just strengthen ourselves enough to *patiently* get through the hard times, we will do well. It's kind of like picking our battles and not making too much out of the daily trials.

This would make the good times that much sweeter.

Mother's Book of Home Economics

68

Kitchen Inventory – The Pantry

When we owned our country store, we had to keep track of our inventory. We did not want to run out of things like sugar or canned corn. So we kept a list of all the basic items we needed. Please realize, this was an old fashioned, *Mom and Pop*, country store with hardwood floors and old wooden shelves. There was no computerized inventory. We did things the old fashioned way. We even had a rotary phone!

This is where I got the idea of keeping a list of inventory for our kitchen at home. However, I only use it as a tool for frugality. I make this list once or twice a month and use it to come up with meal plans to get us through several days without any wasteful shopping. I will explain how this works:

Amy and I Make the List

I sit at the kitchen table with paper and pen. Amy (15) looks through the cabinets, shelves, and refrigerator. She tells me exactly what we have on hand. She also tells me the quantity.

For example - 3 cans of green beans, 28 eggs (she actually counts out the eggs), 10 pounds of potatoes, 10 boxes of pasta, 5 pounds of carrots, 10 cans of tomato sauce, 2 loaves of bread, 6 sticks of margarine, 1/2 can of coffee, 10 pounds of sugar, 20 pounds of flour, 1/2 can of shortening, 1 gallon of milk, 1 can of juice-mix, 10 pounds of burger, 16 oz bag of mozzarella cheese, etc.

Once every item is written down, we begin the process of making menus and creating a small grocery shopping list to make up for needed items (if necessary).

The Menu Plan

- I require counsel for this. (smiles) I always call my oldest daughter, Rachel (22) to help us. I tell her exactly what I have on hand (from the list) and she gives me a ton of ideas for creative, economical meals. Next, I look through my old cookbooks and find more ideas. Then I ask various family members for suggestions, based on the inventory.

As each menu is written down, I *cross off* the exact ingredients from our inventory list. For example - if we make a dinner consisting of meatloaf, green beans and mashed potatoes, I cross off one pound of burger, 1/2 a stick of butter, one can of green beans, 5 pounds of potatoes, 2 eggs, 1/2 a bottle of BBQ sauce, 1/4 of a can of bread crumbs and a portion of the milk.

We keep this up, planning meals and crossing off the needed items from the inventory list, until nothing is left and I have enough meals to get us through the required number of days (such as 2 weeks).

Mother's Book of Home Economics

The Shopping List

I will often need a few items. This might include: 1 bottle of BBQ sauce, 1 gallon of milk, 2 dozen eggs, 2 cans of corn, etc. I will only buy the few exact items necessary in order to FRUGALLY clear out my pantry based on the meals we have written down.

Conclusion

I want to stress the fact that I do not create a pantry list based on things I want, or things I hope to have on hand. For instance, even though we love to make homemade pizza, I rarely have the necessary spices -like basil and oregano. So I end up using only one or none. I do not have the money to stock my pantry with basic necessities. I simply use this inventory list to carefully, prudently and creatively use up what we already have.

**Historical Pantries included canned garden produce, and bulk basics like coffee, grains and sugar. These were mostly farm pantries, where the family was able to obtain eggs, butter, milk and meats from their own animals and land.

Please contrast this with a modern day kitchen - we use the store flyers to stock up on sale items. We also take advantage of "reduced" goods offered for a fraction of the retail price - like yesterday's bread, meat and produce. These food items form the basis of a modern kitchen pantry.**

69

The Wife's Job at Home – Doing My Part

Lately, I have been tired and not really trying hard enough. On the day I should have gone grocery shopping, I only bought a few things "to get by," because I didn't want the hassle of planning a list and buying what we needed. Was I lazy, tired or unorganized? Possibly a little of each.

My husband has worked in retail for almost all of our married life. Whether it was our own store we owned, or working for other companies, he knows a lot about getting a job done. When a store opens in the morning, the shelves need to be clean, well-stocked and everything has to be in its place. The aisles have to be clear of cardboard boxes and totes. The deli/ or kitchen area has to be prepped and ready for orders. In other words, all jobs have to be done!

I cannot tell you how many times my husband has come home from work, telling me how employees - slacked during their shift, killed time, and didn't bother to get all their work finished. This either leaves the burden on someone else to pick up the slack or causes an unorganized, chaotic situation.

Can you guess what I am about to say? What I do, as the wife in my home, is my part of the job in this marriage! Just like my

Mother's Book of Home Economics

husband must get all his work done at his job, I must get all my work done here at home.

If I leave a messy kitchen at night, when I wake up, I will face a nightmare. I will have to quickly clean before anyone can even have breakfast or make coffee. If I don't do the laundry, no one has clean clothes for work or church. I must do my job.

When I am feeling very weak or ill, I have learned to come up with the attitude of "do it anyway." Here it goes:

1. I am too tired to clean. "Do it anyway."

2. I am too bored to grocery shop. "Do it anyway."

3. I am in too much pain to wipe up the spill. "Do it anyway."

4. I don't want to get out of bed. "Do it anyway."

You see, we have so many excuses, so many moods, and so many valid reasons why we didn't do our job. But guess what? If I honestly cannot do my work, then it is my responsibility to delegate it to someone else, and make sure it still gets done.

I love the organized plan of our ancestor mothers. They had a day for each job. It went something like this:

* Monday -wash day

* Tuesday -ironing day

* Wednesday- mending day

* Thursday-shopping day

* Friday-cleaning day

* Saturday-baking day

I don't want to follow a rigid plan like that, but I do need to pick one day a week to do my shopping and make that permanent.

Can you just imagine if we were more focused on our job, and all the tasks that go into making a home, how much more organized and pleasant our homes would be?

Every day, my husband goes to work. He does his job with dedication and pride. Why would I do any less here at home?

70

Beauty in the Home

Looking around right now, I see a home that is "lived-in." What that means to me is that I have not done my work. I have not kept up with things over the last day. I have not made the effort to make things look pretty.

Sometimes, I would rather sit in a comfortable chair, eat *Stella Dora breakfast treats*, drink tea and read a book. But I cannot do that every moment of every day, so I must get up and do some housework.

Cleaning and maintaining a home is like tending to a beautiful flower garden. There might be thorns that harm and cause pain. You might slip on the damp ground, after a storm, and get hurt. You might need to use some extra strong soap to get rid of all the accumulated dirt. There is *labor* behind the beauty. This labor is literally *hard work*.

But even in the process, we can create peace and pursue joy. We can smile and take the time to do our best work. We can add a few extra touches here and there to go above the call of duty. We can work despite the grumpiness of human nature that surrounds us.

Just a few minutes ago, I decided I had to get my work done. First I went to the shelves of our library and selected a sermon to listen to. I found "In a Father's Footsteps" by Charles Stanley. I will listen to this in the kitchen while I *clean* and *sparkle,* and then plan our supper. I will also choose an extra pretty apron to wear. I think I will use my Edwardian Apron this time. I will also put on the pearl necklace that Nana gave me the other night, remembering the importance of classy homemaking. It will add just a little touch of class to my outfit. (I am wearing a skirt, top, sweater and *slippers.*)

Making preparations for my work puts me in the right mood to delight in homekeeping. There is beauty in the Home, but only if we make it happen by our efforts.

Mother's Book of Home Economics

Do We Really Care About our Homes?

I've seen beautiful estates, with lush landscapes. They show pride of ownership. They show a *distinction* and an honor for "home."

There are those of humble means who have a sense of pride for where they live. They do their work each day, to keep things clean and neat. (Even Ma Ingalls swept the dirt floor of the soddy house.)

I don't understand why society encourages people, in this day, to be casual with their chores. They encourage them to have messy, "lived-in" homes, and laugh at piles of dishes. Unless there is illness of the caretakers in that residence, it shows they don't care about their home.

If we really cared about our homes, we would make sure we did our laundry and our sweeping and our dusting and our washing. We would do our dishes and clean our kitchen counters.

I wonder if this has to do with the *abundance* in American culture. When we are overwhelmed with "too much," we tend to do "too little." If we have too many distractions, or too many possessions, it can be crippling. The abundance must be dealt with, so that we can focus on the problem, and then the solution.

Forgotten Kindness in Marriage

There is a joke that once a couple gets married, all the nice gestures end. Things like opening doors for a lady, or baking a favorite dessert for a gentleman, just don't happen anymore. Why is this often the case? Because so many worldly cares come in and rob us of our best behavior. We get caught up in trials and worries, and have trouble taking the time to do nice things for those in our own homes.

Lately, this seems to have happened in our house. Mr. White and I have been on **alert-mode**, solving problems. There has been little time for slowing down. Today, we had a lovely time annoying each other (smiles), and then apologizing.

Then he made the first effort. . . He turned on "The Waltons" on Television. He knows I love that program. He would never watch it, *unless he was being nice to me.* I was grateful. Later, while I cleaned the kitchen, I asked him if he would like something to eat. These were the little gestures of affection that we had been neglecting.

It was time to shut out the worries, the problems, the trials, and just slow down our home life and be *nice*.

Then we took a drive to the hospital where our *second* grandchild had just been born. We both held the new little treasure. It is a girl, and she is very precious. When it was time to leave, Mr. White opened the car door for me. I was content and happy.

It only takes a few minutes to swallow our pride, control our temper, and be *nice*. These little sweet actions can help make a marriage a precious, cherished institution. It also makes home a little heaven on earth.

73

Creating a 1950's – Like Childhood

When I was a child, we spent most of our time playing outdoors. We would head over to a neighbor's house, walk to the corner store, or head down to our small, private beach at the end of the road. Often children would gather in our yard and we would play games like:

1. Red Rover.

2. Freeze Tag.

3. Kickball (we had four trees in the yard, conveniently set up to make a square- which was perfect for bases.)

4. Dodge Ball.

5. Races

We would also ride our bikes and roller skate in the street. We could all walk to the elementary school and use the playground, tennis court, basketball court and baseball field.

One of my favorite things to do was take a blow-up raft (boat) and use that at our private beach. We also enjoyed skipping rocks in the water and running in the sand.

Summer time would mean outdoor picnics, and the neighbors would sometimes stop by to talk to our parents and share a little food and drink. There was always homemade ice cream. We loved watching Dad make it. He would use dry ice and a hand crank on some kind of bucket. It would produce sweet, cold vanilla ice cream!

Dad would buy a large watermelon and store it in the downstairs fridge. We would wait for days, excited for when we could eat it. "Dad got a watermelon!" We would say with delight! Then on the day of our fun, we would sit outside at the picnic table and enjoy our delicious treat on paper plates, after having hot dogs and hamburgers.

Sometimes, Dad would surprise us all by saying, "Let's go! Everyone in the truck!" We children would climb in the back and hang on. In those days, it was okay to sit in the back of a truck without a seat belt. He would take us to the next town and buy us each a soft serve ice cream with chocolate sprinkles! We were carefree and happy!

In the winter, many children would gather in our yard to go sledding down our hill. We had the best time in the snow and we also enjoyed making snow angels and playing until it got dark. Then we would be so cold, we would head inside to warm up by the fire to drink hot chocolate and have our supper.

Mother made supper every night around 5 p.m. That's when everything quieted down. We were healthy and happy and worn out from our playing.

Mother's Book of Home Economics

This was a 1950's style childhood and I want to create it for my own children. When I was growing up, we did not have computers, cell phones, or any other contraption that kept us occupied in the house. We wanted to go outside and create our fun. In this current society, we have to *help* create this for our children. We need to get outside and teach them how to play red rover. We need to work on making our yards the fun place for the neighborhood children to enjoy. We need to make home a safe and happy place to be.

74

Why the High Cost of Food?

We have become a nation who eats *recreationally*. It is part of our "entertainment" expense. We have snacks and processed food and junk, because we like the taste of it. We are kidding ourselves if we think snacks are good nutrition.

In my childhood home, grandmother* would have a *fit* if we kids were offered ice cream before dinner. That wasn't allowed. Grandma made simple homemade meals, with little meat, all week long. Sunday dinner included meat as the main dish. This was common in those days.

When Grandma passed on, my mother continued with the common tradition of making sure we ate nutritionally. We had a home-cooked dinner every night at the same time. There were no snacks to hold us over until the meal was ready. We greatly appreciated the food when it was served because we had time to become genuinely *hungry*.

The only time we had snacks was on Friday nights. We children all looked forward to the homemade popcorn and a little soda. We would watch a program with Mother and Dad on that night and enjoy a special time together. If there was soda in the house, on the weekends, we were allowed only one glass. After that we had to drink water.

Mother always had orange juice and milk in the house. We drank the milk with meals and the juice in the morning. These were not all-day-long beverages to enjoy. They provided a certain amount of nourishment that we needed. But overdoing the nutrients was a waste, because the body could not use it.

We had plenty of tea and water available throughout the day. If we children wanted soda (other than on Friday night) we bought our own, from the local corner store, with money we had earned ourselves.

If we wanted extra snacks, candy, or junky convenience foods, we bought it on our own. I still remember my pink, homemade bookcase that My Father made me. It was in my bedroom and that is where I kept pop tarts and the occasional treats I would buy from the store myself. This kind of junk was never in our kitchen cabinets. Mother knew it did not satisfy hunger. She knew it did not provide basic nutrition, so she didn't buy it.

I remember babysitting, as a young teenager, and finding cabinets full of hostess snacks, chips and cupcakes! I couldn't believe it! It was exciting! One family, in particular, was a mother and father who had a baby. I was the babysitter. When the parents left, I checked the kitchen for snacks and couldn't believe how much junk food they had! It was only two adults and not even any children, and they were eating all those treats themselves! This was obviously for entertainment. It was for enjoyment. I knew it did not provide any nutrition.

In other countries, throughout the world, people eat basic foods like whole grains, potatoes and locally grown produce. If we gave them a box of highly processed American snacks, what do you think that would do? How do you think they would feel?

In the old days, Mother would serve oatmeal, or porridge in the morning. She would serve homemade cornbread, biscuits or bread. She would cook with homegrown potatoes, carrots and onions. Her seasonings came from the garden. I don't think her fruit trees produced BBQ potato chips or candy bars.

We have become a nation who expects junk on a daily basis as if it were a necessity. This kind of eating makes us unhealthy, broke and unsatisfied. It reminds me of birthdays. When we give our children presents all year long, buying them some of the things they want, rather than waiting for their birthday, they become selfish, and think people "owe" them things. They don't learn to wait. They don't learn to delay gratification. They don't learn to work for things. Every single one of us will appreciate things more if we have to wait for them.. . To earn them. . Like ice cream (smiles). . . I remember watching my father make homemade ice cream outside. He had a large bucket and had to crank the handle for a long time. He worked to make the ice cream that we got to enjoy. We appreciated it very much! But I don't think I appreciate buying a carton of ice cream from the supermarket.

Now I must say, if you looked into my shopping cart today, you would find junk. . . (sigh). . We are *all* going to struggle with this because it is such a normal, expected part of our diet! But this is something we all have to fight. This is something we will all struggle with. Because if we keep giving-in to buying and eating the garbage, we will be broke and diseased.

* Grandmother - Our family lived in the same house with my grandparents, just like my parents now live here in my home with my family.

75

The Housewife Contract

When Mr. White asked me to marry him, I hesitated, then stated my one *condition*. I asked that I be allowed to be a housewife and never have to go to work. He agreed.

I didn't realize until many years later, how important that promise, that contract, meant to our lives. We have talked about it over the years, laughing, smiling . . . despite hardships, good times or bad. We always went back to that day on the Pier, at the ocean, when he promised I could be a housewife. He promised to take care of me, and our family. This happened in the 1980's. Many women were working. While there were still housewives in my neighborhood, the majority of wives held jobs outside the home. But my personal yearning, was to be a wife and mother. That was all I ever wanted out of life.

In this modern society, we are told that very few women are housewives. Frankly, I don't agree. There are many women committed to staying home with their families. There are even women staying home, tending to the house, being hospitable and taking care of husbands, even though they have never been blessed with children. Yes, it is okay to stay home even when there are no children, or when the children have grown!

I came across some sweet quotes, in my reading this week:

"My Mother's occupation and hobby, vocation and avocation was motherhood."

- Mary Higgins Clark (the famous suspense author) speaking about her own mother in "Kitchen Privileges," her memoir, page 32.

"Mom never worked a day outside the home. We were her life. The house was always clean and comfortable, and she would always be baking cookies or bread or making something special for us to eat. When I went to college near home, I could count on finding her there, cooking, reading, knitting (needles and yarn were always close by or in her hands). She made an immense impact on our family."

- John MacArthur - Servant of the Word and Flock – (from his biography written by Iain H. Murray, page 11)

Mother's Book of Home Economics

Mrs. or Miss and Other Titles of Respect

In ballet class, the students are required to call their teacher "Miss" and then her first name. This shows classical respect. This was also common manners when I was a child. A Friend who visited was called "*Miss* Annie."

If it was a very close family friend, one who was beloved, she was given the title of "Aunt." I had a few "Aunts" who seemed like they were part of our family. I would not have ever dreamed of calling them by their first names without using the title "Aunt." (My own children have a dearly loved "Uncle" who is my husband's closest friend.)

We had visitors from the south in summer. The small children would call me "Ma'am" even though I was their cousin. It was because I was their elder. Have you ever heard a sweet child with a southern accent call an eleven year old, "Ma'am"? It is precious! The children would never say a simple "no" or "yes" without a "Ma'am" or "Sir" when speaking to the older generation. It was common courtesy. (*The adults responded the same way, as an example, by saying "Ma'am" and "Sir" as well.*)

In those days, the world was *family* - centered and *adult* - centered. Children were cherished, but were taught to give up a seat for an

Mother's Book of Home Economics

older person. When company came, they would gladly give up their bedroom for the guest. The children would sleep on "pallets," or blankets, on the living room floor. They were happy with this arrangement and knew no other way. Children looked forward to the privilege of being grown and looked forward to growing up and getting to be an honored adult.

Children were also taught to "go play" during adult conversation. Parents and visitors would talk quietly about the news of the day, or some trial in the family, so as not to upset the innocence of children. This was part of respect and manners in the home. Children did not live in the adult world. They were honored and protected as children.

One of the greatest blessings in life was to *earn* the title of "Mrs." Girls were called "Miss" until they married. I remember being called "Miss Sharon" growing up and I loved it. There was some dignity and elegance to the title of "Miss," just like in ballet class. If I was helping in Sunday School, the little students called me "Miss," or "Ma'am."

But when I became "Mrs. White" I was honored and delighted. Suddenly I had protection, in a sense. I had a covering and a very special reason to act accordingly. I had a husband who expected me to be a lady, and an honor to his name. Women used to proudly address themselves as "Mrs." . . . When out in the stores, they would say hello to each other by showing respect to the family and husband by saying, "Hello Mrs. Smith! How are you today?" It brought out the grace and dignity in all. (*Of course, in close, personal visits, first names were used.*)

When titles are used, it brings out gallantry in gentlemen and refinement in other women. In the old days, no one scoffed at titles like they do today. This is part of the reason we have an extremely casual self-centered society. No one wants to give place to respect and honor.

In the old days, Ladies dressed like ladies. They were in skirts and dresses, not sweatshirts and sweatpants. Women and Children dressed up to go to the store, the church, or out visiting. We presented ourselves in our best because this brought out the best in others. Ladies also gave their best to their families, at home, by dressing nicely. They did not wear ratty, casual clothes. They would wear a comfortable, but pretty, house dress with an apron over it. This meant they cared about how they looked and wanted to please their families by looking sweet and pleasant. They were also ready to greet unexpected guests. This does not mean they were in their Sunday best, but they looked nice and were not embarrassed when someone came by. This carried into their homes.

When we use Titles and Have Respect and know the place and the value of Manners, we not only look nice, but our homes look nice. We also treat others in a more civil, kind way. We respect the family, the institution of marriage, and the love of home.

One of my greatest wishes is that they would do away with the term "Ms." because it brings confusion. Originally, we know that Miss means unmarried and Mrs. means married. Why then the term of "Ms."? I would also love if unisex clothing went out of fashion. I would love if our town and our state and our county realized the

Mother's Book of Home Economics

potential for traditional royalty and started to act accordingly. Truly this would trickle down to our children and succeeding generations and bring more pride and love for values and manners.

Recently I saw a picture of a modern family. It was a Husband and Wife with all their children. They were dressed up and smiling. Even though they looked lovely, I could sense a casualness to them. I contrasted this with an early 1900's historic photograph (in black and white) of my grandfather when he was a small boy. His siblings and parents were also in the picture. The dignity and pride came through in their stature and poise. Their clothing was amazing, even though they were far from rich. This was the traditional family of which I speak. This is where titles and manners and customs of the old days brings out the richness of our heritage.

If only more ladies were proud of being called "Aunt" or "Miss" and thought it endearing. If only neighbors and friends were commonly called, with a sweet smile, "Mrs." If only children were taught to give up their seat for their elders and learned to honor them with titles. While the adults, likewise, protected their innocence and taught them by example. Maybe we could recapture the joy of family and understand that royalty and dignity is possible, once again, in this great nation.

77

It's Time to Make the Rooms Shine

I spent *hours* sitting by the window this morning. My only student sat nearby. We had blankets and pillows and piles of books. It was a studious time of enjoying literature. After awhile, we had beverages and toast. Then it was time to get to work.

I put on my apron and assessed the condition of the kitchen. I piled dishes in the sink to soak in hot, sudsy water. Then I decided to clean the parlour instead.

I lit a *mint-chocolate-chip* scented candle. It sat next to my forlorn, wilting flower plant. (*A gardener, sadly, I am not.*) Then I got the pledge and a dust rag. I polished the end-table. . the lamp. . the large table, the hutch and the wood pellet stove. Then I dusted the window sills.

I dragged in the large vacuum cleaner. It is a charming pastel green. I vacuumed the carpet and then started on the kitchen floor. It reminded me of the old days. In my childhood home, we had a large, round throw rug that needed to be brought outside to be cleaned. This covered most of our living room floor. It went over the linoleum. Most of the house was plain linoleum. We had to sweep all the rooms. I don't even remember using a vacuum cleaner.

In my mid-teenage years, when I worked as a maid, I was intrigued by vacuum cleaners which had a "floor" setting, along with a "carpet" setting. We used to vacuum all the wood floors and all the linoleum. It made things very quick and easy.

Today, as I worked and *remembered*, I started to vacuum the baseboards. This too was quick and easy. Smaller boards, and those in corners, were done by hand, with the use of a rag.

I then swept the hearth, *washed my dustpan*, and tucked in all the chairs. The room looked lovely. I went to the back door to get a better look. All was charming and shining and pleasant.

Then I remembered something. . . my kitchen was still a mess. I had plenty more work to do.

78

A Vow of Poverty

It always happens. . . We Mothers start building up our savings and something comes along to take it away. But most often, the need is for those around us, especially our own children.

Godly Mothers and Fathers often make a subconscious vow when they start a family. The vow is one of poverty. This means they pledge to spend the majority of their money on the needs of their children. (*"Needs" not "Wants."*)

We never see these kinds of mothers in costly array, or in fine homes. We don't see them shopping idly in boutiques, or dining in elegant restaurants. These mothers use their material resources to care for the poor, and the needy, even if that is often their (old or young) children.

Old Time Mothers in poverty would scrimp and save and find ways to make sure their children had decent shoes, nutritious foods and a humble home.

When money came in and was saved for a rainy day, Mother was delighted to have the cash to feed a hungry, weary soul, who had entered her cozy parlour to take a break from the painful world.

All money that is used for selfish needs, all health that is consumed to glorify self, all worries of reputation fall by the wayside for the godly mothers. She seeks not her own gratifications.

The vow of poverty is not a promise to live a *destitute* life. It is a pledge to use all that goes through her hands, to bless and encourage those around her.

If I pledge my "wealth" and my "health" and my "reputation" for the ministry of my own family and for those that come through my door, I have made a vow of poverty for the Lord.

This means I will *spend* on that which is eternal. I will find a way to *serve* despite my health issues. I will not care what *others* say or think of me, but only care of the view from God's eyes.

Mother's Book of Home Economics

79

The Old Time Housewife

Before American Feminism took root in the 1970's, women looked forward to marriage, family, and a home of their own. A Girl would spend years learning to cook and clean and take care of a home. She might gather special things for her future life. She hoped for a future as a wife and a mother. When that day finally came, it was like her graduation. The moment she stepped into her first place, whether an apartment or house, she got right to work.

She dressed nicely, did laundry, baked, cooked, grocery shopped and kept a nice home. She catered to her husband and followed his wishes, just like a secretary would assist her boss. There was a mutual respect and admiration - each contributing much needed skills to the marriage. Each had their place.

These old time housewives took great pride in their work. And they were *grateful*. The husbands wanted their wives at home. One common saying was heard by these good men, *"I don't want my wife working."* A husband wanted the home *kept*. He didn't want his wife running around, getting into trouble, gossiping, or working to earn the living. He wanted his wife dependent on him, which in return helped make her sweet and gentle and thankful. If she became discontent with the income he earned, or tried to run out and earn the living, she was usurping his authority - she was criticizing his role. A good wife learned to adjust her housekeeping to the lifestyle her husband provided her - whether in a small, humble cabin or a grand mansion.

A wife who was sheltered and protected in the home, *the kind who loved being there*, this wife was the joy of the family. Her sweet spirit was surrounded by her loved ones. She was there for all their troubles and turmoils. She was there to nurse them from the pain of the world. And they dearly loved her! She was not distracted by schemes of getting rich, or finding herself. She was not lured away by the local mall or the endless luncheons put on by women's clubs. She was home and happy and cherished. *Why was she cherished?* Because she was grateful and humble and willing to serve her family.

When a housewife acts like they did in the old days, eventually it brings out the chivalry in a man. It makes him want to protect and care for her. But her actions must be genuine, and they come from years of trial and error. The good wife is motivated by her desire to do her part, without any reward. But, the reward *does* come.

Something went wrong, over the years, when these old time housewives stopped setting the example to the younger generation. The young people of today prefer sloth, messy homes, and co-habitation over an old fashioned home life. They find no pride in keeping a nice home. I wonder if this is because some feminist came along and whispered in their ear, that the floor does not have to be scrubbed or that it was okay for dust to accumulate. Her whispers

Mother's Book of Home Economics

told the wife that she deserved better and she wasn't being treated right. Feminist trickery was designed to make the wife unproductive and take away her work at home; So she would be free to run around, or get into her husband's business and try to usurp his role. I wonder if these little, subtle steps, slowly eroded the yearning for a godly family. I wonder if this breakdown started with being tricked into running off and neglecting the home.

80

Will You Walk the Grounds with Me?

In Jane Austen's day, guests would "take a turn about the room." Or they would walk the garden. This was a way of visiting. Two or more would walk together and talk. It was a *restful* sort of recreation and exercise.

When the weather is nice here at our Vermont Estate, I often ask one of my teenagers if they would walk the grounds with me. We have a 2 acre parcel of land. I walk up the back property, near the rushing river and enjoy the retreat - like setting. We have a tiny garden plot with new blueberry and strawberry plants which have not yet been established enough to bear fruit. But they are fun to look at.

In the early spring and summer mornings, I do the majority of my housework. I do the dishes, the baking, some cooking, and tidying. Then I do laundry and hang it on the clothesline. While I work, I look forward to my walk around the grounds. I love to call out, on my way out the door, "Will someone walk with me?" Often it is one of my teenage boys who goes with me.

I see things that remind me of what it must be like on old homesteads. In the spring, farmers would walk the property and assess the needs. A certain fence might need to be repaired. A barn door might need a hinge tightened. Perhaps the porch steps need a few boards replaced. The farmers worked hard to maintain and repair the grounds so the homestead would function as it should. On my own property, I see some weeds that need to be removed. I see a porch that needs painting and a playground that needs to be cleaned and ready for children to enjoy for the season.

All these chores can be done at our own pace, over many weeks or months. They give us great joy to labor on our own property. We take pride in our land and our homes, when we enjoy our own work.

As I am walking the grounds, I am not thinking about what must be done outside the property. The outside world is shut out. Peace reigns. A soothing happy feeling of walking the garden with my Lord is in my thoughts. . . *And for just a little while*, I forget about my poverty, realizing I have everything I *need*, in this old 1800's house, and on this beautiful land.

Mother's Book of Home Economics

81

Housekeeping with Mister

It rained all last week. Mr. White had promised to help me start our humble garden, so when the weather cleared a bit, I walked outside with my pink umbrella. Mr. White smiled at me and mumbled that it was *not* raining. I watched while he put soil into planters. My watching is part of helping.

I walked around the 2 acre property, happily holding my umbrella, and standing near him. I followed while he did the heavy labor of digging soil, and clearing bits of land. When he signaled, I dropped flower and vegetable seeds. . . just a few. Gardening is still an experimental hobby for me. I am an amateur and Mr. White willingly helps me. *I wouldn't dream of gardening without him.*

Inside our 1850's colonial house, I cleaned the kitchen, baked banana muffins and chocolate cake with strawberry pink frosting. I vacuumed. . . and dusted. . . and washed all the curtains.

When the curtains were clean, I stood on a chair and tried to reach the rods to put the curtains back on the windows. Mr. White smiled. He is over a foot taller than me. He started to help. We worked together. He got the rods and I filled them with curtains.

Like all people, sometimes I forget to be content. This means to be at peace and yielded happily to one's lot in life. I cannot let the bad days or the normal strains of life make me forget about the happiness of being here. I have to remember the cozy fires and reading books by Charles Dickens. I need to remember the time I have to patiently crochet an Afghan or hand-sew a new apron. I can play checkers or chess with my children at any time. I can bake and cook and serve my family in an unhurried way. I can be here for my children and grandchildren any time they need me.

This morning, Mr. White mowed most of the lawn, while I made a hot lunch. When we took a little break, he reminded me that despite all the troubles, we are very blessed and grateful for what we have, and for our way of life.

The very act of cleaning and cooking and keeping a home reminds one of how very precious it is to have a home and family. . . To be *settled* and *peaceful* is the very definition of contentment.

82

The Foundation of Cleaning

Very early in the morning, I cleaned the main rooms in this large old house. I swept the floor, scrubbed the sink, counters, and stove. I washed dishes, cleaned canisters, and made the parlour look nice. This is the heavy sort of cleaning one does as the foundation of other cleaning. It is the deep down work that makes the rest of the day's work easier.

I will often rearrange the interior of the refrigerator to keep some order. Things should be in their place - the milk goes here; the ketchup goes there. This makes everything easy to find and not strewn about. An orderly fridge makes one pleasant.

The sun is just rising on the front grounds. The windows are open. I will soon sweep the porch and tidy up the outdoors! Cleaning is pleasant work when it is done with skill, purpose, and a little quiet. (*No one is under foot at this hour.*)

Soon the family will awaken. I will hear grandbaby's morning cry in just a few hours. He will want his breakfast and lots of attention. He will want to walk the gardens with grandmother. The children will make most of the meals, and I will enjoy some leisure in the afternoon.

For right now, I will rest content, with a cup of tea, because I have already accomplished a delightful mission in the home - I have done the day's foundation of cleaning.

83

The Estate without Electricity

I was watching an old episode of "The Waltons," late yesterday afternoon. I loved to see their large old house and how productive everyone was at home. There was cooking and baking, mending and sewing, cleaning and gardening. There was always so much to do and so much excitement with a house full of people.

Then I heard thunder outside. A large storm came in and took away the power in our house. This is not normal. We rarely ever lose power, here in the rural mountains of Vermont. Even in the midst of a snowy blizzard, we usually keep our power. It was a little shocking.

The evening hour was fast approaching. Things were getting dark. Mister set up his old lanterns at the parlour table. We sat in the old antique chairs and visited while we waited for our kitchen to start working again. One cannot make tea or treats when there is no electricity for the stove.

As the hours passed, some of the children played cards by candlelight. Grandbaby was tucked into bed for the night. The entire town was quiet.

The sound of the rain was pleasant, but the thunder and lightning was a little frightening at times. Some of us wanted to read, but the dim lights would not give us enough light to see. Someone stopped by to visit. We heard work crews out behind the property. There was some excitement for a little while.

At some point, many of us went to bed. It had been a tiring day. There would be plenty to do in the daylight, even if we didn't have power. Somehow, during the night, it was restored and all was back to normal.

This morning, as I listened to old gospel on my kitchen radio, and worked about the house, I was grateful for our electricity. Yet, sometimes I wonder what it would be like to have all the comforts of electricity, without the dependence on television, computers and radios like we have today. Perhaps that is something that each family can work on, to set rules and limits on their use.

The Amish have rules for the way they live, so that the modern world does not seep in and take away their simple life of service for the Lord. They have boundaries and limits on what they will allow into their daily lives. This reminds me of the resolutions great ministers used to make years ago - Puritan Jonathan Edwards and John Wesley come to mind. They set up plans for their daily actions and lives and resolved to do them. This is what is missing in many of our modern lives. This, to me, is the lesson of the loss of electricity, for those few evening hours. Many of us need to decide, much like the Amish, what will be best for our own homes. We need to find a way to keep resolutions for a godly home, and decide what that means for each us.

84

Depending on Mister

I went out this evening. Mister took me to the supermarket. It felt like I was going into "town" and it felt like an ordeal. I didn't want to leave home, and was weary, but I knew my husband would take care of me. I have been worn out and still recovering from recent ailments. I felt very *dependent* and was so grateful to be taken care of by my family. There is a sweet meekness when one cannot do very much for oneself.

Over the last month, as I have been without my car, I have thought, maybe there is something I should do to come up with money? This is a normal, foolish thought. Immediately, I remembered that the Lord is in control. He has a plan. He is working behind-the-scenes. I will stay back and in my sweet place, where my dear husband has kindly kept me. He is the provider, I am the housewife. (*I shall not be moved.*) I cannot tell you how many times a "sickness" or a "trial" has come my way to slow me down (and get me out of the way), so the Lord could do some great work. In this case, I have learned that being home all the time, and depending entirely on Mister for any errands or outside needs, has been the most wonderful blessing of my entire marriage.

It has created a stronger trust and faith in God. It has made my faith soar. It has taken away MY will, and taught me what it really means for HIS will to be done.

I am a grateful housewife, and find great joy and peace in keeping the home. This means to stay home. No matter what I think is best, no matter what I think I have to do, staying home is the greatest blessing for a housewife.

There is a beautiful quote by Elizabeth Prentiss (1800's), which describes it best:

"As for her, like most women, she had but one ambition. To be a good wife and a good mother, and to be beloved by her husband and children, was all she asked. [She was] a busy, affectionate, cheerful little housewife, whose voice would never be heard in the streets, but whose memory would always live in a few faithful hearts."

85

No One Respects Homemaking Anymore

The telephone rang. . . I spent 10 minutes in idle conversation. Finally, I politely interrupted to say, "*I have to leave on an errand in about 10 minutes, but have to finish up my housework first. I'll have to call you back later.*" But my phone guest wouldn't let me off the phone. Has that ever happened to you?

I had spent the morning dusting, polishing, vacuuming, doing dishes, taking care of the laundry, and fixing meals. The rooms were almost sparkling. I had just one more section to vacuum and a couple more dishes to do, and I would have been finished. I would have been able to go out on the errand and enjoy an afternoon of rest when I got home. Through all my work, I had chatted with my husband and children, helped them with their needs, set up the schoolwork for my youngest student, and had some helpers working with me.

When phone guests take up more than a few minutes, it can derail our efforts in housekeeping. I asked my guest, "*If you were at your job when I called, and you had to get back to work, would you let me keep you on the phone? Or would you tell me you HAD to go.*" The guest and I laughed. I then said, "*No one takes homemaking seriously.*"

The fact is, if you are a housewife, you are in charge of the care and keeping of the home. It is **your** responsibility to make sure the rooms are not dirty and that they are periodically cleaned throughout the day. Just as employees at a company must do their assigned jobs. This is serious business.

I have heard the joke about stay-at-home moms. It goes something like this....

A career mom stops by to visit. She notices the house is in shambles, and everything is chaotic. Her snarky comment is, "*Oh. . .* I thought that since you were home all day, your house would be clean."

Have you heard that one? How often is it true?

People must understand that we often spend a few hours each day cleaning the house. We can't allow general (non-emergency) interruptions to distract us so much that we become procrastinators. We have to politely limit our activities enough so we can get our jobs accomplished each day - Just like a professional.

It is also important to rest, but we must be diligent in our work. My children are amused when I tell them I am on a break from my housekeeping.

Our breaks are like sitting on the front porch with a little lemonade, enjoying the afternoon sun. We are ready for visitors, or idle conversation as a form of *refreshment* and *fellowship*. But this is after our work is finished, or during our rest periods.

We, *of course*, are always available in an emergency and will drop whatever we are doing when needed. But in our normal daily life, we need to be about the business of housework.

86

Building our Homes with Little Money

I grew up in the same house my mother grew up in. It was a beach cottage that Grandpa spent years rebuilding, while Mother was a small child. By the time I arrived, it was a large 2 story house with enclosed porches and an efficiency apartment in the basement. It had charming French doors and windows in the living room, which led out to one of the porches. There were stone steps and a small decorative fence on part of the property, close to the lilac bushes. Not only did Grandpa rebuild the house, he also cultivated the land, creating a garden, and encouraging the growth of lovely plants.

Part of the foundation of the house was on a mine of rocks. These rocks were in a section of our basement, piled high, with the house built on, and around it. The rocks were also on the great hill beside the house. This hill has been covered with dirt and grass and was a wonderful place for children to play in both summer and winter. We sled down the snowy hill, or rolled down the grass in the nice seasons.

I used to watch Grandpa working on that hill with his tools. He was covering the rocks, or working the land in some way. This was when I was a very small child. (We children lived with our parents and grandparents in the same house, just as my parents now live with my family.)

Years later, I learned that much of the supplies and lumber Grandpa used to rebuild the cottage was from salvaged items found on the shore of the nearby beach. This was typical for a generation of hard working Americans who knew how to find necessary items and create things with very little money. But this wasn't just the Depression-era Americans.

Remember when Pa Ingalls would build an entire cabin out of the woods? He would cut down trees and work with the land to coax it, and to create, *with his own labor and skills*, to make a Home for his family. In these days that would be called "scavenging," But it was the *normal* way.

Now we buy everything at the local hardware store or lumber yard. I was thinking the other day how much I want a glass, French door for one of our rooms. I had thought for months about going to the store and buying one. But where is the fun in that? I would rather wait and search for such a treasure, scavenging it just like my ancestors did a few generations ago.

I remember when we lived in Massachusetts and I had gone into this thrift store, when my children were very young. I found a white wicker shelf unit that was faded and worn. I brought it home, set it up on the porch, and spray painted it a glossy sage green. It looked beautiful! It dried on that porch in the lovely sea air, since we lived near the ocean. Later, when I set it up in the house, it brought something artistic to our home, *something amazing*, because I had taken special care with it. It probably cost me around $4, including the paint, and I loved it.

If we can only look back at our American History and understand how homes were built using labor and local resources, rather than spending thousands of dollars at the local shops, we could have a stronger sense of appreciation and pride. We would gain a tremendous ability to survive. The money we could save, over the course of a few decades, *and the example we set*, would create a precious inheritance for the next generation.

87

Singing Comfort to Baby

Late yesterday afternoon, I brought grandbaby out on the front porch to see the pouring rain. Our Vermont acres look like an English garden, or an amazing view of an Ireland landscape. The rain was soothing and quiet.

Baby is 9 months old and is teething. He was fussy in the house. I wanted him to be distracted by the fresh air and pretty views. He loves my front porch.

I sang "*Amazing Grace*" to him, slowly and softly, while I paced the porch. He was happy and content. Then I rang the bell, which is right near the sliding door on the porch. Baby looked at me with wide eyes and then smiled. . . A few minutes later, one of my sons appeared from the back yard, thinking I had called him. We laughed. I was just showing baby the fun things at the Estate.

I sang to baby some more, about faith in the Lord, and eternal matters. He listened and looked at me, while we walked the porch and enjoyed the rain.

I remembered when all my children were babies. I always sang to them. "Bringing in the Sheaves;" "Trust and Obey;" "Shall we Gather at the River;" "When the Roll is Called up Yonder;" are some of the many hymns I sang to them, over and over, throughout their babyhood and growing up years.

There is peace and joy when one's heart is at home. There are heavenly matters to pass on to the next generation, from a quiet heart, who isn't distracted *or overly busy* with outside cares.

Teaching babies about our Heavenly Father, can easily be started with simple songs, and joyful hearts. *This is the most comforting thing to little souls.*

Mother's Book of Home Economics

88

Ex – Housewife

The other day, Mister had to fill out a jury duty questionnaire. When he was finished, he left the papers on a desk for me to mail. I glanced at the part where it said, "Name of Spouse," and "Occupation of Spouse."

Here is what he listed as my job:

"Mother and Housewife."

I was delighted and proud. This is my lifelong vocation. I have a home to care for. I have children and grandchildren to tend to. I am my husband's companion. *I keep the home.*

Today's homemaker often has a home where everyone "does their own thing." Husband and children can microwave their own food. They are capable of doing for themselves, after all. They can clean the house, do the laundry and anything else Mom can do, right? Well, of course. But this breeds a home that needs no mother. This breeds the home where lessons of homemaking, and tender mothering, cannot reach the next generation.

My boys (16 and 20) were talking about working mothers. I said, "I could never leave this house. I am needed here." I went on to talk about all the things I do, and the *just being here.* One of my sons said, "How would we ever eat well if you were not here to take care of us?" Now this son is an amazing chef himself and a hard worker, but he appreciates having Mom home to keep the house and prepare special meals. Yes, he can do all these things himself, but why would one want a home without a full - time homemaker, a full-time mother? *The family needs a dedicated mother to make the home a place of rest and recovery.*

I realize there are mothers in terrible financial circumstances who currently work. Many want to be at home. *But there are many more mothers who **choose** to go out to work because they want to.*

Some mothers had been home while the children were young, but then decided to go back to work, or got bored and wanted something new and exciting in their life. This is called an "Ex-housewife." This term breaks my heart. It makes me think of a broken home and an ex-family. It makes me think of a home that fell apart because mother left.

The older Christian mother is to be the example to the younger generation. Her staying at home, often waiting through the seasons and phases of life, faithfully loving and tending the home, is to be the ideal example to the young Christian Mothers. What breaks my heart is that many of these Titus 2 Mothers are abandoning the call of home and becoming "ex-housewives."

Scripture says for us to be ye separate. We are not to mimic the actions and ways of the world. If there is a mass exodus of women into the workforce, why would the Christian woman join the crowd and leave the home?

Mother's Book of Home Economics

Is it hard to stay home? When there are financial trials - YES! Upper class housewives have it easier than the rest. They *worry not* about money. But the majority of Christian Homemakers work harder than most people by making food from scratch, laboring in the garden and home and taking care of the family. This is hard work. But it is a precious calling. It is a normal way of life for the sweet mothers of yesteryear. We can keep this going, from generation to generation. But we must learn to never take on the title of being an "ex-housewife."

Mother's Book of Home Economics

89

Overcoming Hard Times with Grace

In this economy, many of us are struggling. There is a confusion added to this, about standard of living. We see magazine covers at supermarkets of *beautiful* homes and *elaborately* prepared foods. We see television programs about rehabbing houses, and making them "livable" with the latest upgrades. This is like an upgrade in standards, and it costs far more money than most of us can manage.

It used to be that thrift stores and churches had decent clothes available for free, or for a meager cost. Many mothers used to talk about the *missionary barrel*. When times were hard, they would find clothes and remake them with what they had at home. They made lovely things with their own efforts, out of cast-offs.

Mothers were able to create recipes based on *what was left in the pantry*, rather than what was for sale in the store.

Home repairs and maintenance was done to survive, with scrounged supplies, or inexpensive parts to make-do, for those with little money.

I realize we need certain skills to create out of little, but we can certainly learn.

Money used to mean something different than it does today. Money was for basic housing and basic needs, and an occasional treat, rather than for splurging and spending on what we *want right now*. [Or what we *think* we need in this confusing, consumerist, culture.]

We need a good dose of the history of the family during hard times. We need to read about the depression-era mothers, the pilgrims, and the pioneers to find a way to overcome the culture of today, with dignity and grace.

90

Living Without Credit Cards

I don't think we realize the extreme poverty that is hiding behind the modern credit industry. American culture is under the illusion of wealth because of our growing consumer debt.

There has always been 'credit' and 'debt', but not the dependence on *credit cards* to survive. This is what frightens me.

In the early years of my marriage, credit cards were rare. We all waited for the next paycheck, or the next month, before we bought items that weren't essential. We had our budget for food and rent. But things like clothes, home decor, or gifts were not part of the financial plan. We had to save and wait to buy those things. I remember waiting an entire year before we finally got curtains for our apartment. If we didn't have a bed, we slept on cushions on the floor.

If we needed shoes for the children, and didn't have the money, we would go to the local thrift store and see what we could buy, using some scrounged-up change. (I remember taking a nice new looking pair of shoes, and trading them for a smaller pair, in my pre-schooler's size, at the local thrift store.) Sometimes, this got us through a month or two before we could buy the necessary new pair of shoes our little ones needed.

Our family is from a wealthy town in suburban Massachusetts. We are used to all the shops and malls and restaurants. Going to "Brigham's" for ice cream after a movie was part of life for the young people. Spending money was the way we lived. We all worked hard and earned what we spent. We teenagers did not borrow money from our parents or even have an allowance. We all had ways to earn a small income - through jobs, babysitting, yard care or whatever we could do. The idea of credit cards or borrowing money never entered our minds. I didn't know this kind of thing even happened until many years into my marriage.

The only consumer debt I was aware of was a layaway plan at the local K-Mart or Ames department stores. We mothers would wait for a good sale, and buy the items we needed for our families, including gifts and clothes. We would pay a little each week, without interest or obligation, until our items were paid for. THEN we would receive the merchandise. Or, if we decided we couldn't afford our things, (perhaps a problem came up) we would cancel the layaway.

There is a common type of debt that occurs in life, which includes emergency car or house repairs. For us, these kinds of things are rare, but every company has worked with us to come up with a payment plan. We did not need credit cards for this kind of debt. These bills were always paid off within a few months. However, it always put a strain on our budget. We would cut back on other things to make the payments. It is impossible to get ahead in life when we overextend ourselves financially.

Patience and going without are crucial for the working class.

Mother's Book of Home Economics

There are many times in my marriage that we have lived in utter poverty. These struggles taught us valuable financial lessons. We appreciate everything we have. We know how to live with very little. We have never raised our standard of living, even when Mr. White's income has increased over the years. We have only lived in cheap apartments or bought homes with a tiny mortgage. We live simply so we can survive the rough times.

Have I ever used credit cards? Of course. I hate them. They are dangerous and devastating. Currently we have no debt (other than our mortgage). We don't own a single credit card. We don't want anything to do with them. They enslave us. They train us to depend on them for our existence. By having everything NOW, and not waiting for it, we slowly build up a burden of debt and misery that very few can ever escape from.

I would rather go without. I would rather wait for the treats and the *seeming* necessities. I would rather have this historical, working class approach to spending, than live with the illusion of having what I want now.

Even though it may seem harder to live without credit cards, it is the most freeing, amazing, peaceful financial experience you could ever imagine!

91

Cleaning House with Baby

It is certainly a challenge to keep house, when there are babies and small children around. But these are *the loveliest times of all* for the homemaker.

Babies often look on curiously at all the work we do in the home. They are shocked by the noise from the blender, the vacuum, and the washing machine.

One day last week, I was making a cake. I had grandbaby in the carriage. He watched as I brought down the large mixing bowl (to his level), and used my electric hand-mixer to stir the cake batter. He loved it!

I have put him in the walker while vacuuming the carpet. It is easy to play fun games with baby, when one is cleaning. He enjoys seeing all the action going on at Grandmother's house.

We garden together, hang clothes on the line, wash dishes, sing hymns, sweep floors, and wash the high-chair tray! *Well*, I do all those things while baby *watches*. (*Much like when I am helping Mister with his stuff, He does all the work, while I stand nearby.*) It's really the being together that is wonderful.

Part of playing with babies and children most certainly happens while we are living our normal, daily life. We just bring the children along in our activities, making our work and our days *delightful*.

92

Electricity as an Entertainment Expense

Many things we use today for recreation are run with electricity. We watch television, DVDs, play video games, listen to stereos, and use computers. In many homes, there is more than one television set in use at the same time!

We also tend to (unknowingly) be more wasteful. We leave too many lights on, overuse the clothes dryer, and use far more water than necessary.

There was a time when electricity was only considered possible for those who had money to spare. Air conditioners, fans and even electric refrigeration was foreign to many struggling families up until the mid 1940's.

There were other ways to entertain oneself before the days of excess electricity consumption. My childhood home had a large piano in the living room. We children had such fun with it, even though none of us had formal lessons. We also spent many hours outdoors - playing, running, riding bikes, having get-togethers, doing yard work, dreaming, visiting and enjoying the fresh air.

When someone, in my childhood home, was ill, a small portable television set was brought in for their use while they were bedridden for a day or two. This helped keep them comfortable and entertained while they recovered. But it was not normal to watch lots of television, or have more than one unit running, in everyday life.

Something that might contribute to overuse of electricity is the lack of hard work being done in, and around, the home. Years ago, we would see mother sweeping the porch, hanging laundry on the line, gardening and cleaning, or decorating the home. She would wash windows (both inside and out), polish patio furniture and clean out the car. Dad would be seen playing ball with the kids, mowing the lawn, doing house repairs, and taking pride in the way his house and yard looked. Parents found joy in taking care of the house, which made the short time of evening recreation more valuable.

I wonder what would happen if we limited the use of electricity during daylight hours. We could use those hours to be *productive* and *creative*. When the sun sets, we could use the *unnecessary* types of electricity that we all enjoy - for computers, television and the like. This would seriously reduce our electric bills! But most of all, it would simplify our lives and make it more rewarding.

Mother's Book of Home Economics

93

Basic Cookery

I studied cooking in Home Economics classes when I was a teenager. My mother also gave me freedom in her kitchen. I would look through her cookbook and bake special treats when the pantry ran low. While Mom did most of the cooking, I was happy cleaning and cooking whenever I got the chance.

In my first home, I enjoyed making meals for my husband. I still remember our first trip to the local supermarket. We were so excited to pick out our own groceries, *together*. I made his breakfast, packed his lunch, and made his dinner each night. With a small household, and a decent income from his job, we didn't have much to worry about financially.

As more and more children came into the home, I had to learn to make many things from scratch, with the ingredients I had on hand. I remember going to the local library and finding all kinds of old cookbooks. I borrowed them, and found recipes that would work well for my family. Many of these recipes (like breads and stews) were made so many times that I memorized them. If I really loved a borrowed cookbook, I would save up and buy my own copy.

Frugal, or thrifty, cooking is a valuable skill for the housewife. People often share recipes, which is good. However, many families have different tastes. Some have allergies. We also live in different climates and have a different cultural basis for what we eat. In the Boston area, fresh lobster and clam chowder is common, whereas, they may not be staple menu items in a little town in Idaho. Restaurants in Florida serve the most delicious fresh orange juice you could ever taste! They are known for their oranges and have them in abundance. We have to make use of what is available and low cost, in our area. It is important to learn how to adjust recipes to work in our own kitchens.

It is a common cliché for mothers to save money by serving "rice and beans." This might work for many, but not in my house. One cannot always save money by doing what the masses suggest. We have to remember to serve foods that our own family will enjoy. Cooking basic foods from scratch will save money. Serving carefully portioned- sized- meals and storing leftovers will also save money.

To learn basic cooking skills my favorite book is "The Good Housekeeping Illustrated Cookbook." It boasts 1,400 recipes! The pictures are stunning and are set up almost encyclopedia - like. My children used to love to look at all the pictures and say, "Let's make this one!" You will learn to make easy breads, muffins, meats, and all kinds of dinners and desserts. Once you learn the basics of these foundational recipes, you can start adjusting ingredients to meet the needs of your family.

Basic cooking also means you have freedom from the supermarket sales ads. Certainly buy hamburger or chicken only when they are priced reasonably. But you can make so many different things with them. The store will recommend processed foods to go with the meats. Cooking from scratch means we don't need those items. You will no longer be a slave to what is on sale.

When we buy hamburger in a "family sized" package, I take it home and divide it up into smaller portions. I then put each meal's serving in a gallon Ziploc bag and freeze it. Even though we have a lot of people in this house, I only cook with that small amount of meat. It is the ingredients that go with it, that make the meal stretch - the vegetables, the bread, etc. I love the older cookbooks from the 1960's that have old menus that go along with the recipes. This was from a time when portion sizes were much smaller than those of today. The fun in the dinners had a lot to do with the beverages, the way the vegetables were prepared, and the lovely way in which it was all presented.

Nourishment was key, and homemade was the most nourishing of all.

I realize we mothers have days of being exhausted and can't do as much as we would like. But when you are in the habit of cutting and washing vegetables for stew, or whipping up a quick batch of muffins, making food from scratch can be a valuable part of the daily routine. When all my children were little, I had lots of helpers. We set to work at the big kitchen table. I had children rolling out dough, or peeling vegetables. The bigger children were at the counter or stove stirring sauces, or handling the hot foods, while the *safe* work was done at the table. Meal preparation was a happy, pleasant way to pass the time with small children. To them, it was playing! It got the work done, and the children enjoyed it. They also loved taking turns serving the food and giggling and visiting at the table.

These days, I have a barstool in my kitchen. I often sit near the counter to wash dishes, or to make biscuits. I also have my kitchen radio nearby to hear CDs of gospel music or sermons. Often my grandbaby is in the highchair watching me work. He plays with bowls and lids and has a wonderful time. The kitchen can be a happy place to be, making frugal cooking a pleasant part of life.

94

The Other Side of Motherhood

We live in a generation where everything seems to happen instantly. People can often make things work *fast*, or right away. Things are *forced* to happen "on time," in many cases. This takes away our patience, and even our attention span. Sadly, over the last few decades, this has trickled down to the expectations of mothers.

We do our best to raise our children to be good, moral citizens. We want them to produce the fruit from our years of hard work in teaching and training them. We expect them to make the right choices and the right decisions. This shows us their maturity and wisdom. Yet, it isn't really about us. It is about God's timing and God's will.

In the old days, Mothers knew to wait out the seasons and the phases. They knew there was a point to stand back and let young ones make decisions. They knew to let the children face consequences; in order to learn the lessons and to grow and mature.

This became very clear to me the other night. Some of my older children came up with an idea. I was tired and said I couldn't help. But I was there to observe as the events unfolded. I knew what the result would be. *I was excited about the lesson they were going to learn.* This time, no matter how tempted I was to interfere, or make their lives easier (thinking they had endured enough and had done enough), I backed off and let it all happen without me. I did not give advice. I did not take over the burden. I had tea, went to bed early, enjoyed a quiet night, and I prayed for them. The following morning, the results were in. They learned the lesson! They got the advice from the *experience*, instead of from my words!! It worked! I was delighted!

Many years ago, I read something about Mrs. John R. Rice (the wife of an evangelist and mother of six children). She talked about her children having meaningful work in the home. She said chores taught them important lessons. One day, one of her girls was very tired from a hard day at school and work. But it was her night to wash the dishes and clean the kitchen. Mrs. Rice was so tempted to go in there and say, "*You go rest. You did enough today.*" But she stayed back. She said she wouldn't dare take away that lesson! Her wisdom astounds me.

Mothers, in this generation, have spent much of our years interfering with God's lessons for our children. We have gone in there and tried to "help" or "ease" things. This is part of control. This is part of *impatience*!

When we observe the lives of godly grandmothers, we see a peaceful patience, and a knowing compassion for the young. They don't give up easily on the youth of today! They know there are phases, and trials, and mistakes that must happen to bring forth a mature adult.

Mother's Book of Home Economics

Lately, I have seen my grown children come out of some tough years. I have seen a "light" of maturity and peace coming from their lives and actions. There are difficult teen years and young adult years for most (if not all) children. But once they pass over that rugged hill and rough patch, they will emerge as an incredible blessing to their mothers.

The other side of motherhood, is from the grandmothers. We look back over the years and see how quickly it all really happened. We see patterns and lessons and trials. But none of those "moments," or phases, lasted too long. Some took hours, some months, and yes, some took years, but the children made it through. We mothers of today, must stand back and have great patience and faith. We must trust our prayers to reach the Master, and know that it will be okay in the end.

95

Financial Survival in Hard Times

I don't think we realize how bad things are in this economy. Many of us have decent homes to live in and cars to drive. We even have furniture, computers, telephones, electric appliances and cable television. While we suffer without much money, we are able to enjoy some home comforts.

But things are getting worse. The cost of food and gas is skyrocketing. Yesterday, I drove to the grocery store and had only $32 to get through the week. I had to decide which meat to buy. I needed 4 meat items for 4 suppers. Then I needed eggs and bread. I still have some food at home, but needed to supplement what was already there. I had to buy a small can of coffee, rather than the large one I normally buy. When I got home, I reminded my husband that we must ration the rest of the sugar and all the coffee. It had to be enough to get us through until the next payday.

I quickly made a simple supper - hot dogs and beans. I did not have macaroni and cheese to go with it, like we normally would. I ended up making a small batch of chocolate chip cookies so they would feel like they had a treat. I also announced to the family that "there is popcorn you guys can make later, in the air popper. There is butter to go with it." Then I made a batch of iced tea.

And that was our night... *Tomorrow*, I thought... *God would provide for us again tomorrow.*

Granted, we have enough money to pay all our bills. Yet that leaves us short for food and gas. It leaves us without any extra money for little bits of happiness - like buying an ice cream, or nice cold soda on a warm day. These treats help cheer the soul. . . Now we must find another way to find that cheer.

Times are going to keep getting bad. In light of this, I wanted to share with you a few ways I have learned to "go without."

1. I love Mary Kay, Avon and other name brand skin care products. But I don't use anything more than a steaming hot facecloth, and a little moisturizer to care for my skin. (No toner, No skin cleanser. . nothing.) I have been doing this for many years.

2. I buy make-up from the dollar store. I use it for months and months until it is gone. (I don't care that the experts say to replace it every 3 months.)

3. I wear torn and ripped up nylons almost every day. But you can't really see the rips because they are too high up. When I have a little extra money, as long as the children are happy and don't need anything, I buy a new pair.

4. My skirts, tops, dresses and sweaters (I never wear pants - they are too casual for me) - are purchased at nice stores in the mall - on clearance in February and March each year. I pay anywhere from $3 to $7 for each item. There are no thrift stores near me. We are in a very rural area.

Mother's Book of Home Economics

5. I don't eat much. Most of my grocery shopping is for foods the children and my husband like to eat. If money is very tight, I will eat oatmeal, toast, hot tea, water and cereal for the day and be just fine. When there is money, I enjoy chocolates and cookies. (This might explain why the mothers during the Great Depression were very slim.) If I am really lucky, I get to enjoy a Freschetta pizza - my favorite!

6. I drive very carefully. If you go at a steady speed and avoid lurching, speeding up or suddenly slowing down, you can conserve gasoline and make it last much longer.

Jobs are scarce. Many are out of work. Life is harder in America for a generation that is used to consuming and enjoying pleasant treats. We are in a time where we must learn to be creative and survive on less.

96

The Breakfast Hostess

From a very young age, I had my girls doing housework. They were such sweet helpers!

When Nicole (now 20) was 10 years old, she was in charge of the morning work. This was because she was an early riser. This sweetie, used to get up at the crack of dawn, sit at the kitchen table, and do all her homeschool assignments before anyone even woke up!

Her title was: **The Breakfast Hostess.**

Here is what she had to do:

While we were still sleeping, she would set the table, pour drinks and prepare breakfast. It could be as simple as cereal and juice (most often) or as complicated as a Pillsbury Quick bread (the only thing she could bake at the time). Once we were all called to the table, she, as our breakfast hostess, had to wait on all of us. Did we want seconds? She was to serve us. Did we need a spoon? She would get it. It was like she was a pleasant waitress who took care of us. Her job was to make sure we were all happy and enjoyed our breakfast.

Her manners were impeccable. Do you have any idea what it was like to wake up and find your smiling daughter, standing by the table asking you if you were ready for your tea?

The final portion of her job was to clean the kitchen. She had to clear the table, wash the dishes, and sweep the floor. Then she was off duty for the rest of the day. Rachel (my oldest) was the *Lunch Hostess*.

Now that both of these girls have grown up, I only have one daughter left to help me with the kitchen. Tonight, Amy (14) was our dinner hostess. She cooked the entire evening meal, served us at the table and then cleaned up the mess. I was very grateful!

97

When There Isn't Much

When someone would get a new apartment, we'd go take a look and start cleaning it. We'd all pitch in and get that new home ready for the family. Sometimes that apartment wasn't much to look at. But with all of us cleaning, we'd make it look pleasant and happy.

There are times in life where we take a "step down" in our standards. These are times when we have lost much or are just struggling. We have to live in a smaller home, or deal with a broken-down car. The best way to deal with this is to look at it as an adventure. Remembering, that we still have our skills and talents.

Years ago, when our family owned a country store, I would sit behind the cash register, in the evening, while some of my younger children would play on the front porch. My husband would be working the kitchen, making food for customers. It was a small town and the community was wonderful. I would sit back there and hand-sew while I waited for a customer to come up to the front register. Our home was upstairs in an apartment. I used to sew for a few of the people. Someone needed mending, another needed a hem taken care of. I did it in a motherly way and didn't want money. We had moved from a grand neighborhood in suburban Massachusetts. We experienced major culture shock when we moved to Vermont. But this was not a step down. Life was entirely different, but better.

I like to think of Ma Ingalls and the many times Pa had the family move. Ma would make do living in the wagon, while she waited for Pa to build a house. She would sweep the dirt floor, and use her homemade quilts for bedding. She had very few possessions, but made each home cheerful because she kept things clean and neat. She also kept a routine. Those children knew what to expect. They had regular meals and chore time and play time. My own Mother has made a home in many places and has always added nice touches here and there, even without money.

It used to be that when a bachelor got married, he loved the daily nurturing tasks a woman brought to the home. She would fluff pillows, make beds, sweep floors, iron curtains, and make the meals look pleasant. She added life to the home with her creativity. She added rainbows and cheer with her attitude and acceptance of what she was provided with. She made things go far with what she was given.

Wherever we go, wherever we live, regardless of our circumstances, we can manage beautifully in a tent, a cabin, shack or house. We can do this with our talents and skills. Have you thought of how "The Swiss Family Robinson" survived on an island? They were inventive, creative and used survival skills to manage each day. It is certainly not the ideal, but we can cope and cope beautifully in most situations.

Mother's Book of Home Economics

This very thought, *survival*, can make us so grateful for each day. It gives us the motivation to get up and make a lovely breakfast, clean the house, and get all dressed up. We can serve our family in love and devotion.

But when depression hits and makes things very difficult, *as we dwell on our suffering*, this is the time to get out the Bible and read the Psalms for comfort and guidance. This is the time to sing from the hymn books and to listen to the old time sermons. This is the greatest comfort you will ever find.

May your homes be like little sanctuaries of happiness and godliness.

When Mother is a Shut – In

Life has been very quiet here at the Estate. I have been cooking and baking and keeping house, at a slow, peaceful pace. I have not been able to leave the property. We have no car and no public transportation, in our rural area. Mr. White is getting rides to and from work. It has now been 2 weeks since I've been able to attend our beloved Church. Our car is in the shop and we don't know *if* or *when* it will be repaired.

I have loved staying here at home. It has been a great blessing. It has also been an important lesson for me: Staying home, *for a wife and mother*, as much as possible, is the greatest thing she can do. Why? Because she is creative at home. She is not harried or under pressure from constant errands and outings. She can cook from scratch more and monitor the economy of the kitchen inventory. Her sweet presence in the home is invaluable to the family for a great many reasons.

Staying at home, for a homemaker, is part of the job description. The reward is incredible!

Yet, there are still the worries without a car, even if it were just for Mister. We must have a running, dependable vehicle. We must. There are groceries to buy, banking to do, and a job for him to get to.

Today, I had a sort of childlike wonder about it all. I trust the Lord. I know He is doing some great work. So I willingly yield to this trial, *making do* and bringing as much light and joy into my home as possible, while we wait.

My mother-in-law used to keep a running note on her fridge. She rarely left home. So when she was almost out of laundry detergent, trash bags or milk, she would write on a note on the fridge. I never heard her complain or panic about running out of milk (like I am sometimes tempted to!). Papa, her husband, would pick those things up at the store on his way home from work, on a certain day of the week, or *when he had time.*

My pantry is running low and I wonder when I will get to the market. A few days ago, I made chocolate chip muffins. I used apple juice instead of milk, because I knew I couldn't spare the milk. Yesterday, I made my sons Macaroni and Cheese, but we had no milk to mix in with the powdered cheese. So I used a little spring water instead. It turned out just fine, and the boys enjoyed their lunch. If I didn't know to do these kinds of things, I would not be able to calmly make it through this trial.

Something amazing is up ahead for us. I believe it. . . We've had many rough financial times, and this year is no exception. But we've been down this road before. I have seen miracles and been greatly blessed by them. Today, to keep a holy faith, I pulled out my favorite children's books: "Uncle Arthur Bedtime Stories." I will read these in my parlour chair during homemaking breaks. I will read about sweet families who prayed and pleaded with God for their daily bread. Tears will fall as I rejoice with them, as God works in mighty ways! These are true stories written by Arthur Maxwell, and are gems! Reading these today, will encourage me in my own prayers, and help me on my walk to victory.

99

Mothers with Christmas Courage

Tonight is Christmas Eve. The stores and banks will close early. Families will be gathered at home, or visiting one another. There will be church services tonight and everyone will be pondering the birth of Christ and enjoying the Passages from the book of Luke. It is a heartwarming time of year.

Yet, in some homes, there are financial woes. When these mothers think of Christmas, they despair at the idea of coming up with money for presents. They pray and cry out and wish they could afford gifts for their children. Perhaps the heating bill was too high this month? Or the car was acting up? Maybe the cost of basic food is getting to be impossible to manage. Regardless of the source of their worries, these mothers cannot imagine Christmas morning without some sadness. They hear others say *their shopping is done* and *the presents are wrapped*, and they weep in their hearts, because they have not.

We must remember that many years ago, this mass idea of multitudes of presents was not the normal custom. Remember Laura and Mary Ingalls? They received an orange, some Christmas candy, a knitted scarf and a Christmas penny. They were thrilled and delighted!

Alas, we want to buy our children nice things. We love them dearly and enjoy seeing their happy, surprised faces when they open gifts! We have to be ever so careful to come up with the money and choose just the right items. The depression-era mothers would spend months filling up their money jar, scrimping and saving so they could buy a special gift for each child. It was an enormous sacrifice, but one these mothers would willingly make.

I remember, years ago, when I only had two little girls. I stayed up late each night, all week long, before Christmas and sewed matching dresses for my children. I used a dark calico print with pretty pink hearts all over it. I trimmed the dresses with lace and made matching hair ribbons. My girls were so surprised and wore them to church on Christmas morning. It was such a sacrifice for me, but worth every moment!

In these hard times, Mothers of today must have courage. We walk into our kitchens and wonder what we are going to feed the family. We have to smile and pray and come up with creative ways to make nutritious, filling meals. We need to keep the thought of hardship, suffering, and *want* out of our homes. Our children need to feel secure. We must be brave and inventive! We have to avoid giving-in to depression or sorrow.

We Mothers in this generation are facing hard economic times. I pray these Mothers have *Christmas* courage. It is a special kind of courage and will carry us through for months to come!

100

Money Can't Fix Everything

It has been very cold in this house the last few days. We have been supplementing our heat with a small portable electric heater. I move it from room to room to take the chill off. Our wood pellet stove is broken again. This puts me into survival mode. But Money can't fix my problem. For the next few days, while we wait for repairs, we have to find ways to keep warm and productive in this frigid house.

This morning, I read a little from "We Had Everything But Money." This kind of literature cheers me up and inspires me when hardship comes. One section of the book was written by an author who grew up here in Vermont. She talked about the food stamp program. In those days (the 1930's), going to the town for assistance was something to be avoided unless there was no alternative. The town would write down all the food money that was given to an individual and then publish it in the annual report for all to see. But here is the most interesting part - every single penny that was given, was really a loan and had to be repaid!

She also said the staple diet for most people in those days was - "bread, milk, pea soup, johnnycake and oatmeal." In another section of the book, they talked about eating hot biscuits for lunch. There was certainly very basic eating going on compared to today.

Our health can also affect our ability to survive. About a week ago, I had a minor household accident. While I was cleaning one evening, I slammed into a corner of a piece of furniture. This left a miserable bruise and made it difficult for me to walk for several days. Mother is now incapable of doing very much. The house is going to suffer. Can money fix that? Can money make the pain go away or make me well? Of course not. This is a temporary hardship, like the broken stove, and we must have patience to survive this with grace and dignity.

When we are cold, perhaps we will bake something, or light a candle (for some kind of substitute for the idea of warmth). We will layer our clothing and sip on hot tea or hot chocolate. This is part of surviving. Living here in New England for my entire life, I am used to the frigid temperatures. It doesn't mean I always like it, but it is something I have learned to endure. Struggling with cold winters makes us stronger and more creative.

Physical ailments are also the thorn of my life. But these things can't get us down. We have to realize that bad things have always happened. They are happening now, and they will always happen. We can't dwell on them. We can't gripe about them. We have to find a way to be happy despite the hardship. This has nothing whatsoever to do with money. It has to do with the will of the mind!

Mother's Book of Home Economics

Home with a Grandbaby

Last week, Mr. White and I became grandparents for the very first time. Our daughter had a difficult labor and delivery. She had an emergency c-section and it was frightening. I stayed at the hospital most of the time, to help.

Now that we are home again, we are catering to a patient and a baby boy. It is difficult to maintain some sort of homeschooling routine for my one remaining student (15). John has been helping to cook and to serve meals. He also does much of the housekeeping, with my help.

We are focusing on medical care, baby care and hospitality for the occasional visitor. But the baby and mother must have a routine. I like to remember the nursemaids from the old days, in the wealthy families. Babies got the "air," each day. They often rode in a lovely "pram." They also had their play time (awake time), naps, baths and constant meals and changings.

I am remembering all the things I used to do when my own babies were little. This is a precious time. It is also fleeting. Enjoying a new baby, and all the growth and changes that will happen, is an incredible blessing and a privilege.

We are all very grateful.

Walking the Grounds with Mister

I was walking the grounds with Mr. White, *in the early evening*, here in Vermont. We checked on the strawberry plants up on the hill. We paused to watch the rushing river behind the property. Birds were chirping, as we felt a gentle breeze. Earlier in the day, I had helped plant radishes and spinach in a small raised bed in the front garden. *(My helping means I stand there while he does all the work.)*

Throughout the day, we had good-naturedly annoyed each other. *This is what best friends do.* We *annoy* and we *laugh*. After decades of marriage, we understand communication. We know to laugh instead of taking the jokes too far. We know to make light of home life.

Mister led me to the picnic table on the front lawn. He had spent the day mowing our 2 acres. We were enjoying the reward of all his work.

Rain started to fall. Somehow, I managed to talk him into carrying me back into the house. This is something he will only do for me once a year. *This was the perfect time.*

We made it to the front porch, as rain poured down on us. It was time to get back to indoor housekeeping. Dishes needed to be washed. Supper needed to be made. I had laundry to fold. But I was smiling and happy. Our outdoor adventures on this cool summer day had been peaceful and pleasant. Somehow I had forgotten about my broken down car, or being "trapped" at home. I forgot about the bills, and the stress of life.

We are enjoying the beauty of our Estate and waiting out the *financial thunder and lightning and downpour.* And as we wait for the storms of life to pass, we wait joyfully and patiently for the next step; for the next orders from the Lord. *He* will provide and take care of us. In the meantime, I will walk the grounds with Mister and Keep house and I will be grateful.

103

The Excitement of One New Dress

In my Mother's day, children normally had three outfits. The saying was: "*One in the drawer; One in the wash; And One on your back.*" There were seasonal shopping trips to get a new dress (or outfit) at various times of the year. But it was nothing like today's shopping frenzy, in the modern home.

Before the "requirement" of walk-in closets, people generally had few outfits. They had what was necessary along with one or two special (dress-up) garments. There was no need for large closets. It was not a standard feature when building a home.

When young girls were learning to sew, they were excited at the idea of shopping for material, notions and a basic dress pattern. They would spend hours cutting pattern pieces and fabric. They would carefully sew, and try on portions of the dress. A tremendous amount of effort went into making such a dress! There was also much pride in the finished product. Those dresses may not have cost very much, but they were treasured by each amateur seamstress.

I still remember how much time went into making my very first dress. I also remember selecting a pattern for a baby dress when my first child was only a few months old. I loved sewing a dress for her, and trimming the collar in lace! I have made many girls' dresses over the years and those dresses have been cared for and enjoyed more than any store bought item. Why? Because so much time was spent on their creation. Most of the dresses were made for a specific event or holiday, but worn many times, over many years.

Of course, in this present day, it is very inexpensive to buy a new dress. Sales at local department stores and the quality of items available at consignment and thrift shops make it very easy to find affordable clothes. But sometimes I wonder if we buy *too many* dresses?

What if we carefully sought out only one dress at a time. What if we bought one dress each season, or *made* one dress? Would we take our time and make a deliberate selection, rather than just buying whatever was available (or easy)?

Imagine how exciting it would be if we shopped for *one* pretty dress just like girls of yesteryear searched for a pattern and fabric? Not only would we save a tremendous amount of money, but we would slowly build a lovely wardrobe of charming clothing!

104

Home as a Little Christian School

In this modern day, the worldly culture has seeped into our homes. It doesn't belong there. Home should be a little school of Christian living. Here is where children see Mother and Dad read the Bible, say prayers, and model good manners and morals.

We should also see great industry. We should see cheerful and happy workers in Mother and Dad. They set the example. Dad often takes great pride in the care of the home and yard. We may see him mowing the lawn, repairing porch steps, working on the car, and fixing screens. He is busy with making the property look pleasant. He maintains the little Christian school called "home."

Mother is busy with preparing meals. She might be mending a torn curtain, ironing shirts, washing the floor, or baking pastries. She does this cheerfully, happy to be doing a great work for the Lord in the little home.

Along the way, children are added to the family. They walk beside the parents. They help in the care and keeping of that little school at home. They join in the prayers, the Bible reading, and happy chores. Often young children find chores pleasant and fun because they get to do them with their parents, whom they love and admire. They enjoy the company of the parents and want to do the work along with them. Through this, their own good manners and morals are developed.

Home should be a place which is not a stumbling- block to sin. There should be no liquor, no drugs, no crimes happening (little thefts within the family), no lies, no scantily dressed residents, and no evil or inappropriate television shows. The family ought to take a stance against the world, and stand for a godly home with good policies and rules in the little school at home. Mother and Dad must model this behavior and set the example.

There is a culture of the world's school, in some homes. This does not build the Christian family. Here is where the world's ideas and theories are paramount. Modern parents often buy their children gadgets and gifts and trips to make them happy, but don't ask the children to work for such frivolity. Bible reading or prayers don't happen because modern parents are often embarrassed by it, or their children roll their eyes when it is offered because this is not the kind of little school they attended. It is foreign to them. They were trained in worldliness, amusements, taking it easy, and enjoying being "young."

Mother and Dad must set the pattern in little Christian homes. They must study Scripture and pray and immerse themselves in holy living. This is what will bring a light of wisdom and beauty and godliness into the little school at home. Family Altar, Sermons, Memorizing the Bible, Modesty, Patience and a Servant's heart should be modeled by the parents. This should be done *every* day. This is what makes a happy, joyous home, when Mother and Dad have a heart, and a love, for the Christian School. It ought to be their life's work, their hobby, their everything.

This modern culture is heading to a great ruin. Let our little homes be strong Christian Schools, and let us bring hope to a dying world, by living heavenward lives, even if our little school is the only one in our community.

105

Walking the Gardens with Baby

I had my little grandson with me. He is 9 months old, and such a happy child. There was a sweet warmth in the Vermont air. I picked up baby, and brought him out to my gardens. Now, if you came to my house and looked at the grounds, you would see something far different than I do. You would see a 3 story house that is in serious need of painting. You would see old porches and tired steps. You would see little *attempts* at gardening throughout the land. But the world, as I see it, is a great Estate for us to explore. . . *for baby and me.*

I showed him the lonely strawberry plants beside the front of the house. The soil is not happy there. The plants need to be moved. But we checked on them anyway.

Near the tired porch steps, there are 4 new rose bushes. (Mr. White had planted them for me this past Mother's day.) I was surprised to see that flowers were starting to appear. Baby delighted in my happiness as I explained it all to him.

We walked to the front and saw the lilies had stopped flowering. These had been vibrant orange, sparkly white and robust yellow! But the flowers had gone away, leaving only the green leaves and a memory.

Mother's Book of Home Economics

Next, baby and I walked up to the back hill. There are the blueberry plants and 2 happy strawberry plants. There are several strawberries ripening and waiting to be picked!

Near the hill is a sweet, rushing river behind the property. It is framed by pretty trees and lots of plants. There is a beautiful scent of the outdoors which make one happy.

Baby and I walked to the sad part of the land. . . Mr. White and I had planted starter seeds inside egg cartons and put them in our little greenhouse. Just like we did last year. But a storm came, with lots of wind and rain. The next day, we noticed it had fallen over and egg cartons were upside down in the grass. Baby and I like to visit that spot, each day. I say to him, "I wonder if my spinach will still grow?" He smiles at me and wonders what I am talking about. But I know, someday, we will have carnations and hollyhocks growing up with the grass.

106

The Homemaker's Despair

On Friday, I was given the grocery money. I carefully put aside a small portion for savings and then planned what to do with the rest. I checked the ads and made my list. I bought extra bags of flour for baking muffins, pizza dough and biscuits. I bought marked-down meat for stews. Everything I chose would require more work from me.

When I finished the shopping, I was *discouraged*. I knew there was a week full of hard labor waiting for me at home. I knew it would take tremendous effort for me to make the food last and make sure my family had nutritious meals. I was devastated by the cost of groceries and I almost cried.

Sometimes I think about the families who happily enjoy a night out at a restaurant. I think about those who can buy anything they like. I remember the old days when we used to order pizza once a week, but that no longer happens. Yet, I have to realize that my work at home - the hard labor of endless laundry, scrubbing, sweeping, cooking, baking and washing is the greatest work a mother can have. I am living the life of my ancestors and I have it far easier than they ever did!

It was hard work that built the characters of the citizens of this nation. It was sacrifice, service, endurance and patience that created virtue in the mind and heart. Mothers who kept the home running with their own hands were the hearts of this country.

Instead of being a wimp, I have to feel honored and brave! I have to gratefully work hard and thank God for my lot in life. I need to boost morale in the family. I need to be the example of virtue. I need to smile through my work and make it look fun, much like Tom Sawyer did when he painted the fence.

The other day, Matthew (18) was using a mop to wash the third-floor staircase. It is off in a corner behind our kitchen. John (13) heard the noise and came running. "*What are you doing?*" He asked his big brother. "*It looks like fun!*" Can you imagine that? We about died laughing. But it made me realize something. . .

Home should be full of laughter in the midst of labor. It should be the place where we faithfully work, side-by-side, as a family to keep the home running.

Instead of being in despair at all we have to do today, let us find ways to make it look fun. Let's make it a *delightful adventure*. It will be something to write about in the history books!

Mother's Book of Home Economics

107

Rainy Day Money

Children of today have large sums of money at their disposal. This is compared to previous generations, when having a nickel or a quarter gave one a sense of wealth.

Many of our youth watch commercials, read newspaper ads, and spend an appalling amount of time in stores and malls. They are bathed in materialism.

Young ones used to be taught to "*save for a rainy day*," or to spend months earning the money to buy their own special things.

Each time they were paid, or given a small financial gift (such as for birthdays or holidays), the money went into a piggy bank, or into a passbook savings account. Children delighted in seeing their money grow. They eagerly worked hard to save and add to their modest wealth. This brought them great pride and a sense of well-being.

Daily life was centered around home, school and church. Trips to the store were rare. No one ever went to browse or "hang out." That would have been a ridiculous waste of time.

Mother bought essential groceries, like milk, eggs and bread. She also bought sugar and cocoa and made her own cakes and cookies.

Children were delighted with the wonderful productivity that came out of the kitchen (as opposed to The Food Court)!

Saving money was a duty and a privilege. Younger children rarely had any coins or cash. It was something they earned when they were a little older. This was something they looked forward to, just like doing their part to help support and help the family.

I am frightened that this generation of youngsters has holes in their pockets, but an overflowing closet of goods. How many *things* does a child or teenager need anyway?

Perhaps if we encouraged them to earn and save and have Tootsie Roll Banks full of coins, they would learn the age old wisdom and importance of saving for a rainy day. . . *Sadly, they will never learn this unless we mothers are the example.*

108

Despairing Over the Household Allowance

We are living in very tough times. It takes great ingenuity to make our household budgets work. I read about the Great Depression, and how professors were paid monthly. Their wives would make that money last as long as they could. But by the last few days of the month, they had no money left and ate very little. However, because everyone was in the same situation, it was considered normal. They had a positive attitude and enjoyed their days, despite the *end-of-the-month* poverty.

We all have our good and bad months, and even our good and bad years, financially speaking. Yet this is nothing new to our country or to our world. In History, we read about the very plain and seemingly boring foods families ate. They had things like porridge, bread and milk and a little meat; nothing like the feasting we modern Americans enjoy today. This indulgence can get out of control. When money is always tight, and we expect to have cookies and cakes and meat and potatoes on a daily basis, we may suffer from a self-perceived misery.

One of the hardest things a housewife has to do, is create interesting, nutritious foods that cost very little. She needs to make sure the family has that feeling of "plenty" or "enough," and keep their spirits up. There are two ways that might help motivate her in this:

1. Remember that God has the power to give and withhold wealth. He has good reasons for this. We must have faith that as long as we are doing our part, he will provide for our needs. (*For a housewife, this does not necessarily mean she has to earn money. - It means she has to faithfully do her household tasks, and be careful with the funds she is given.*)

2. Look like a million! What I mean is to dress up in nice clothes when you are out shopping. Historically, when a housewife went into town for her marketing or errands, she would put on her gloves, hat, heels and jewelry. She would do her best to look nice. During the late 1930's and 1940's, while this country was suffering from an epidemic of poverty, the majority of women still looked nice on a daily basis. They made the effort and this helped provide a happy mood for them, and for those around them.

Can you smile throughout the day, despite financial worries? Can you spend several hours a day, cleaning, cooking and "slaving" to make sure your home and kitchen run smoothly, so money is not wasted?

When payday comes, instead of despairing over your household allowance, look at it as your weekly challenge! Dress up for the job and get to work making everything last! This is your adventure. Make it look like fun, just like Mark Twain painting that old fence.

Mother's Book of Home Economics

109

Mother's Courage

In Wartime, as sons went off to join the army, Mother's heart would break. She would watch her boys walk down the lane in their uniforms, and she would pray for them.

During some wars, in some countries, terrible things have happened. Family members were taken by enemies, or by soldiers. I have read about wives and mothers weeping as cruel people took away the family.

How do Mothers have enough courage to go on each day?

There are happier leavings. . . . Children grow up and move into their own homes. Another family is established, another home. Mother feels content to see her grown children at peace and being blessed. Yet, she misses that empty spot at the table. She misses those late night talks of all the news as young adults came home from their outings.

Still, there is an emptiness in the heart and soul when family leaves. How do these mothers go on?

Somehow she must keep her routine. She must keep praying at the appointed hour of family worship. She must make the meals, and sweep the floors. Despite her worries and her sadness, she must continue to keep making a home.

Someday, those precious ones will walk back down the lane to see their old Mother. There will be a happy reunion. Someday, that lane may be heaven, or it may be the old homestead, but there will be a time of reunion and all will be well again.

Mothers must have faith and courage that God is in control, no matter how bleak things look, or how many burdens we wallow in. Mother must continue to have a happy peace in her soul, knowing that faith is stronger than anything we see before us.

Mother's Courage will soar, as she focuses on her daily routine in the sweet little home, and in her humble efforts at homemaking.

Her faithful prayers will soothe the lives and hearts of the missing ones. . . For Mother to stay behind at home, keeping it nice, waiting for the return of the family - . . . this is brave and noble courage.

110

Taking a Break from My Housework

This morning, I pulled out my ironing board. It is set up near my kitchen. I am ironing some fabric for an apron I am working on. I have projects, here and there, throughout the house that are waiting for my creative attention. Yesterday, I organized John's (12) room and made it all neat and clean. We had moved some furniture out of there and it needed my attention.

I haven't baked cookies in at least a week. This afternoon, I plan to mix up a half-batch, since I only have a small amount of chocolate chips left. I love fresh baked cookies!

I am making shepherd's pie for supper. This is a recipe my Mother-in-Law gave me many years ago. I just brown some burger, then layer this on the bottom of a glass rectangular pan. I take boiled potatoes, mash them up and put them aside. Next, I top the burger with one can of creamed corn and one can of regular corn. I spread this out. Then I top this with some mashed potatoes. I bake this in a 350 degree oven for about 20 or so minutes, until the top is lightly browned. It's an easy and quick supper to make. I will serve fresh carrots and broccoli on the side.

I have a quick errand to do this afternoon, but I will bring my hand-sewing project with me. I have to wait in the car for a little while, so this will keep me occupied.

Nicole (20) called me from college the other day. She said, "Mom, what are you up to?" I sat in my favorite chair, put down the dish cloth I was holding and said, "I am just taking a break from my housework." She thought that was the cutest thing. She is busy studying, going to classes, working, and thinks my life at home is "cute." She is precious.

I love to *make a home*, throughout the day. I love to invent new ideas to make each room functional and special. I like to plan out nice foods to bake and cook. I enjoy sewing and ironing and I even like hanging clothes on the line. These tasks make my breaks "deserved," or "earned." So when I sit down with a cup of tea and a brownie (or cookie), I am just taking a break from my housework.

111

Breakfast at Home

When our five children got older, they were less likely to enjoy a nice breakfast at home. They were often in a rush to head out the door, or just wanted to sleep late!

Last week, I was watching an old movie, "Love Finds Andy Hardy," (from 1938) starring Mickey Rooney and Judy Garland. "Andy" lived in a lovely house in a charming neighborhood. His Father was a judge. His mother was at home. She cooked all the meals and was a delightful, practical homemaker. What intrigued me the most was how the family sat down for breakfast, *together*, each morning.

The table was set with a sugar bowl and creamer. There were lovely plates, silverware, napkins and coffee cups. The family sat down and enjoyed a nice breakfast together before heading off to work, school, or to start the day at home.

We live in such a rush - rush society today, that I wonder how many families still set a *formal* table for breakfast?

This morning, I think I will do this. I better hustle and get to work! The family will be awake soon.   Perhaps I will bake fresh muffins and set them out on a bowl, in the center of the table, with a nice linen napkin over them? I can't wait!

112

1930's Style Homemaking

The past few days, I have been watching old episodes of "The Waltons" on DVD. I have enjoyed it so much. "Livie" (the Mom) and "Gramma" both work in the house all day. They take wonderful care of the family. They both wear practical dresses and aprons and have their hair up. They are representing the actions and lives of housewives in the 1930's.

I have been so inspired to just have a quiet house. Is it possible to shut off most of the lights and technology for just a few days? I want an old fashioned home. I want to have a lovely living room, neat and tidy. I want to enjoy polishing my furniture and sweeping my floors. I want to have a nice workbasket beside my chair so I can sit with the family while mending, sewing or crocheting.

I want to listen to a nice old fashioned radio program with everyone sitting all around me. I want my children to come to the table for a large, home cooked dinner. And then, I want to joyfully and lovingly clean up the mess afterwards while the children play on the front porch, so they don't get underfoot.

I want guests to show up and I will have tea and cake ready to serve them. I want to enjoy the old fashioned life in this current day and age.

I want to watch more of "The Waltons" and get my inspiration. Then I want to put it into action. Where is my peace? My peace cometh from the Lord, and the old paths. My peace cometh when I am in my place, as the keeper at home.

113

Home Studies in the Evening Hours

In the old days, farm families worked hard on their land. There were plenty of chores for the entire family. Yet, somehow, they managed to do some studying and schoolwork. Since homes were not full of distractions (like television, video games and computers), studying with the family was a lovely way to pass the time.

Today, many homeschoolers use a strict schedule of starting school at 9 a.m. each day. I used to do this when my children were little. As they got into the teen years, life became more complicated. It was no longer the sweet, slow-paced "nursery" phase. In this modern day, we are also going to be constantly fighting to maintain a balance of using technology (being entertained by it) with learning, studying and producing. This lesson must be learned by today's children.

In the last week, with the addition of a new baby in our family, I have been very preoccupied. There has been more laundry, more cooking, and much more work for me. This also means less sleep! (gentle smiles). Even though this is a joyous time, I have been struggling with a way to keep up with homeschooling my 15 year old (John). He needs to be reminded to do his assignments. He needs to be motivated and encouraged to do independent work. Daily I have been trying new methods to get him on track.

Tonight, I think I found a solution. Our spending time together is centered around chores and school. When we are together, it is when we are cleaning or cooking, or he is reading me his McGuffey or a Bible passage. Tonight, even though we were both exhausted after a long day, we sat at the table to do his math lesson. We laughed at all the mistakes we both made. But this helped our analytical skills as we found the mistakes and re-solved them. This is what quality time has become in our home - a time for learning.

Life never lets up. We often say that tomorrow, or next week, we will fix our routine. Or when things calm down, we will get back on track. But life will keep throwing us something new to juggle. The goal is not to wait until things are better, but to do them in the middle of the challenges.

Right now, maybe I can't play cards with John or watch movies with him. But I can do school. School *became* the fun. We are fitting it in, the same way things were done in history; after a long day of heavy chores and hard work. Our home studies are happening in creative ways. They are happening in a simpler way, from a simpler time - by the hearth, with laughter. . . It has become our evening entertainment.

114

Simple Days at Home

Things are very quiet in rural Vermont. Many of us are getting ready for the coming winter. There are pretty leaves all over the landscape. Raking will soon become a family activity.

There is always so much to do, from sun up to sun down. There are children to care for, meals to cook, and a home to clean. We all enjoy having Grandbaby here for an extended stay, along with his dear mother. They brighten the home and keep the laughter going.

I have been teaching baby how to clean. He just turned a year old. I will give him a damp rag and he loves to clean his own high chair tray. He will laugh with delight when he helps me with the work. Throughout the house, baby's laughter awakens a happiness in every heart. *Every home should have a baby.*

Our wood pellet stove has been fixed. Mister was able to take care of it. He has been doing test runs for us on these cool September mornings. I love sitting near the fire with a pleasant book.

The other afternoon, I made a double batch of homemade frozen pizza. I neatly wrapped them in wax paper and stacked them in Ziploc freezer bags. I thought how wonderful it would be if my freezer was full of homemade foods, rather than packaged

Mother's Book of Home Economics

commercial products from the store. A carefully filled freezer of home goods, is something like rows of home canned foods stored away for the coming winter.

I need to set up a little basket near my parlour chair. Socks, in this house, need mending. I haven't mended socks in such a long time, but I know it will be an enjoyable process. Perhaps when Amy (baby's mother) sits with me to chat, she will pick up some of the work, and we can mend while we have our daily visits in the parlour.

One of the greatest things I have learned as a homemaker and mother, is to have incredible patience with life. One must never act on emotion - never in the moment. Time is needed to pray, or to consider. Having simple, quiet days at home, has made this all very clear to me. Through a trusting patience in the Lord, we have a great contentment. Worries tend not to linger. They fade away as quickly as they came.

To keep busy at home, in a slow and simple way, is a wonderful way of life.

Mother's Book of Home Economics

115

Writing out the Old Home Recipes

Some of my grown children are asking me for our family recipes, so they can cook and bake in their own kitchens. It would be very easy for me to write them out on index cards and ship them off in the mail. But how much more fun would it be to make a little handmade booklet of family recipes, cooking hints, and little family remembrances to go with it?

I have some pretty green heavy stock paper. I can use this as a cover. I will fold it in half, to make it resemble a little booklet. Inside will be plain white paper, folded as well. I can staple this in the center to "bind" the book.

To have a little fun, I can title it something like, "Recipes from The White House," or "The Little Book of Cookery from The White House." [*One must find ways of enjoying one's name when the situation arises. - gentle smiles.*]

I have 12 common dinner recipes, several lunches, and a few breakfasts. To this, I will add some baking recipes, and economical snack ideas. I will also write an estimate of how much each recipe will cost.

Yesterday, I had full charge of my kitchen. (*In other words, I did all the work alone.*) I made my boys a nice lunch of homemade pizza. I cleaned the kitchen throughout the day. As the sun began to set, I asked one of them, "*Will you be needing a baked good this evening?*" He didn't know what I meant by that (smiles). So I translated, "Do you want me to bake something for you?" Well, of course He did! I made peanut butter, chocolate chip muffins. Then I told the boys I was off duty for the night and they were to have sandwiches or leftovers if they got hungry later. I walked out of that very clean kitchen, with the dim lamplight shining on those delicious muffins. . . These are the kinds of *memories of home* that my grown children miss.

I think it is more precious to take one's time creating things of lasting value that will be cherished. My book of family cookery will be humbly made with humble recipes. But it will take me a few weeks, as I sit by the window, in great-grandmother's rocking chair, and write out the *history of our kitchen* for the next generation.

Mother's Book of Home Economics

116

Homemaking Propaganda

In our rapidly changing culture, we have to find a way to keep our bearings. Many take vacations to "get away from it all," and have some quiet. We are bombarded with ads, theories, ideas and marketing images. Many of us long for a quiet walk in the beautiful countryside. This can soothe a tired mind. It can remove anxiety and worries. It blocks the "world's" ideas long enough for us to recover and straighten our walk.

There is a dangerous seed spreading across the world's fields. It produces an anti- homemaking propaganda. It puts us on edge. It wants to shut down the home, make it evolve, and destroy the tranquility of the little cottage where the old time family lives.

One needs a "pesticide" of sorts to remove this from the family garden. It is a remedy, or a fertilizer, to help the spirit of homemaking to thrive. We need our very own godly homemaking propaganda.

This can be found in certain television shows (Olivia and Grandma in "The Waltons;" Aunt Bea in "The Andy Griffith Show.") It can be found in old writings, such as the original "Little House on the Prairie" books. It can be found in some modern books. It can be heard on CDs through old time preaching sermons and homemaking radio programs.

It can also be found in those who live it each day. Each time a homemaker cheerfully cleans and cooks and bakes and commits to being a steadfast keeper of the home, she is sending out good propaganda that will help the next generation to have courage and strength to continue.

The homemaking propaganda can often be a living example of Mother at home. This mother is tending and cultivating the little cottage for the old time family. She is doing this on little money and with minimal material goods. She is making a little haven in the midst of a dying world.

May God bring many more like her. And let us encourage the godly homemaking propaganda to help guide those who are losing their way. It is the Titus 2 mandate.

Mother's Book of Home Economics

117

Homeschooling with Grandbaby

We sat in the parlour in our old antique chairs. Baby was in his carriage. My teenage student was beside me. Baby had a little toy to keep him occupied. The children listened while I read, "The Declaration of Independence." John (15) and I discussed a little about our nation's history and the characters of the signers.

Soon it was time for a Math test. John sat at the kitchen table and started his test. Baby and I went into an adjoining room so John could have quiet. I could still see him through the doorway.

I set up baby's carriage near my chair and pulled out a fun game, "Phonics Firefly." This light-up game teaches letters, sounds, spelling and the alphabet song. I went through all the games with him. He heard the letters and sounds over and over again. He was intrigued!

Later, I read colorful books to baby. I enjoy the stories and love to have a young one to read to again. . . Baby listened to our family worship time (Bible reading, hymns, etc.).

We walked the gardens at our Vermont Estate and were delighted to see strawberries ready to be picked. We noticed 2 of the rosebushes are showing white and yellow roses! *Every so often baby hugs me, and pauses to look at me with a smile.*

Then I walked baby over to the high flagpole on the front property. He looked up to see the American Flag waving in the wind. . . Baby sighs. . . It is so precious when Baby sighs.

Regular life is mixed in with our homeschooling hours. There are meals to cook and dishes to wash. I clean bottles and dress the baby. I rock him to sleep, and soothe his fussiness at naptime. My favorite part of the day, with baby, is kissing away his tears.

Our house is full of all kinds of books and toys for children of all ages. While I am finishing up the last years of John's Home Education, I am grateful to have baby here to begin again. Whether baby grows up and goes to a regular school or not is up to his Mother. But anytime he is here, just like regular *daily life* at our Estate, he will always be homeschooled at Grandmother's house.

118

The Cultured Society of Home

In a biography about Abigail Adams, we are told that her father had a vast library, which she used as the main source of her education at home. A home ought to be a place where solid, appropriate learning takes place.

If a family has money, they might spend it on quality literature - classic titles by Dickens or Austen. They might consider it wise to have a selection of titles from earlier days, such as those published by "The American Tract Society." These were Christian stories of faith and family that were often read by the fireside.

We have been told that Abraham Lincoln came from a very poor family. The only book available to him was the Bible - but what a book!

The key in a godly, cultured home, is not just what we "have" but what is not there. If time and money are spent on meaningless trivia or meaningless amusements, one loses the time to invest in a sweet, wholesome society at home. Money is often wasted on consumer goods, including processed foods, excessive toys and technology. This is an *investment* into the type of society you are creating in your home. We must be selective and careful to choose what we want in our homes. When one selects the furnishings or the drapery or the decorations for a home, one is setting the mood for the type of home they will have. Is this not also true for the types of things or activities that go on there?

Mothers can gently lead the family into a sweet and cultured home by her own cheerful interests in that which is good and noble. I understand that the world has seeped into our homes, in this modern day; but Mother's interests can be carefully introduced. Some mothers may listen to a muted version of Italian Opera while she bakes in the kitchen. Others may have a sermon about the family playing in the background while she does the ironing. Some may be reading the Bible, at the kitchen table and sipping on tea, while the children play. Her actions and her interests will seep into the hearts of her family.

The Amish have a way of making homemade furniture and foods that modern families think take too long. The wisdom in the making is that it breeds peace in the heart and provides a gentler way of passing on skills to the younger generation. Time spent doing this type of work at home with our family is precious and will reap goodness.

While we mothers clean and decorate our homes, may we think of ways to create a beautiful society at home.

119

Winter Days at Home

I am mostly home-bound this time of year. The bitterly cold Vermont days make it difficult for me to get out much. This morning, I will read some of Jane Austen's "Persuasion." I have been working on this book for the past few weeks. I read a little here and there. The story is fascinating and makes one enjoy the *culture* of home-life.

I shall have tea in a pretty cup, and have toast while sitting near the heater. We have lost the use of our wood pellet stove this winter. There is a coolness in the house that makes one a little weary. But we will get a new stove for the next season. We are getting by, and will endure this temporary trial, just as we endure all the burdens that come our way - with patience and a hope for better days.

Yesterday, I was in several of the rooms in this old 1800's house. I wasn't sure what I wanted to do. I had suffered an eye-injury in the morning and needed a warm, cozy room to rest in. I went to the third floor and tidied up before deciding to listen to an audio-drama from Focus on the Family. It was Les Miserables. (Radio Theatre) It was *amazing*. It kept me occupied for three hours, long enough for the pain in my eye to subside. I was then able to get back to a slower paced homekeeping schedule.

Mother's Book of Home Economics

Each room that I enter, I see something that inspires me to clean, or make it look inviting and pleasant. *You can always tell when Mother has been in a room, because of those little touches that make home precious.* A home should look inviting and ready for hospitality, even if the only guests are the residents.

We have an abundance of snow outside. Sometimes I wonder what it would be like to spend winters in Florida. But Mr. White assures me that he will fix our heating troubles very soon. He will make sure I am happy and warm in our humble estate here in Vermont. I will be patient and trust him.

Mother's Book of Home Economics

120

Are You Still Tricking Your Wife?

The other day, Mr. White set up the lights on our house. I sat in our living room and visited with him each time he came in for a break. The children were downstairs with Nana baking cookies. It was strange having a quiet house. As the children grow up and move out, we start seeing what our future home will be like. We do not look forward to an empty nest, but we will still have a happy home.

One of the things Mr. White likes to do is trick me. Yes, *trick me*. He doesn't tell me when he has vacation days or time off from work. He pretends he has to work, but when I notice he is extra happy or that he is enjoying himself too much, I will say, hopefully, "You're not working today are you?" He smiles and his eyes sparkle. I get so excited! I am thrilled to have him here with us. He notices my delight and it is like he has just given me a present.

The other day, we went for a drive - my husband and I. We rarely ever go anywhere together. Either he is at work, or I am doing errands, so a drive together is a treat. As we went along, he talked to me about his ideas and plans at home. Then he tells me all his work stories. I sit content and happy in his presence. The snowy landscape is peaceful and pretty. I realize he has been home for several days and is relaxed. He is overly happy. I know something is up. Then I find out he has another day off!

He laughs. He tells me a story. There is a store owner, on the corner in the next town. Mr. White goes in there every day and chats. He buys coffee and gas and talks about work. The other morning, they had a conversation that went like this:

Store owner - "Are you still tricking your wife?"

Mr. White - "Well, she found out about today."

Store Owner - "How did she find out?"

Mr. White - "She gets suspicious when I stay awake, and am too happy."

Store Owner - "What does she say when she realizes you aren't going to work?"

Mr. White - "She gets all excited and happy."

Store Owner - (surprised) "Really? You are very lucky, then."

We stopped at a supermarket and went in to buy a couple of groceries. Mr. White is much taller than I am. I tag along behind him. He looks back and smiles at me. I pick out a cake mix. He finds something in the hardware department. Then he sees one of his bosses. She greets us and asks how his vacation is going. I look puzzled. Then I look at him. She mentions something about him having 5 days off. I am startled. He looks at me, laughing, like the secret is out.

I realize why he tricks me. Every day, he wants to see the excitement in my face; the happiness I have that he is staying home. But he also knows that I am happy to have him here all the time. Even when we both sit in the living room with the children all around us, I will look across the room and say, "I miss you." He looks up, nods and says, "I miss you too."

Even when the children all grow up and move out, we will still be okay. I will be at home like always. I will cook and clean and bake, like always. He will work. I will make the home. And then we will sit in the living room - he with coffee, me with tea. And we will talk about his dreams and ideas. And we will take rides to the store. And he will *trick me*.

121

Amazing Dedication

Somewhere, *in the middle of the world*, a heavenly light shined down on a virtuous Mother. The angels watched, as she walked the earth with amazing dedication to the Lord.

Through her life, temptations came, but could not take her away from her mission. It all started one afternoon, when she shut off the television, put aside a magazine, and vowed to give up her collection of worldly fads. *Something had happened.* The things of earth had suddenly become dim. Her worldly interest had faded. The former things of the heart had passed away. All it took was one little, hesitant step toward the warmth of holiness, and she was overjoyed with a yearning for heavenly treasures.

In Scripture, we are told to follow the Lord with all our heart. There is no room for other loves, or worldly ambitions. There is no room for worldly pursuits, because that would take away the time and the heart from the focus of the mission.

We are told not to turn aside. We are not to become distracted by *the glitter* or the entertainment in this world. This too will weaken the loving heart and take us away from our mission.

All earthly pursuits that are not founded on a godly vision, will be but hay and stubble at the end of one's life.

The holy war, for the virtuous mother, is to recognize the subtle distractions and to have the courage to ignore them. It is a daily battle. One that makes one incredibly weary, unless one is constantly warming oneself by the beauty of Scripture, old time sermons, hymns and solid church fellowship.

What else do you think Susanna Wesley (1600's) meant when she said, regarding the spiritual training of her children, "I have lived such a retired life for so many years. No one can, without renouncing the world in the most literal sense, observe my method: and there are few, if any, that would entirely devote above twenty years of the prime of life in hopes to save the souls of their children." Two of her nineteen children, went on to be famous ambassadors of the Lord. John Wesley was an amazing preacher. His brother Charles wrote some of the most beautiful hymns one could ever hear.

How else could any of this happen without Amazing dedication? Is it painful to say no to the world and all its glitter? Of course! Is it painful and wearisome to stay on that little narrow path? Certainly. But the discipline it takes to make the effort is rewarded and relieved, when the flood of peace and heavenly joy comes in to renew and regenerate the mother's spirit.

At the end of her life, when others look over the earthly possessions of the departed, they expect to find worldly goods to sort. Instead they find a hymn book, and a tear stained Bible (for the path is hard, but worth it). *Everything else was gone.* Because by the time she reached the heavenly gates, all her interests and worldly cares had dropped away. Leaving the beauty of a dedicated life that amazed the souls she left behind.

And this heroic legacy made many want to stand strong for this same cause, the cause of being a holy light in a corrupt world. On that day thousands more virtuous mothers came along and filled her place on this earth. This is amazing dedication because of the AMAZING GRACE and LOVE of our dear Lord.

Now let me ask you this. . . . Are we really *following* him? Or are we like the toddler child who is constantly getting tangled in the weeds of the world?

The virtuous mother craved and loved the church. She loved her Bible above all things. She observed daily religious duties for the sake of her soul. And these small efforts kept her on the holy path. This is what made the light shine down from heaven. *And the angels watched* and were blessed by her life.

Index by Topic

Etiquette

Finances

Holiness

Homemaking

Hospitality

Kitchen

Marriage

About the Author

Mrs. White is a housewife and homeschooling mother of five children, and a grandmother of two. She is the granddaughter of revival preacher, LD Murphy. She lives in an 1800's house in rural Vermont.

For more titles from The Legacy of Home Press, please visit:

http://thelegacyofhomepress.blogspot.com

Made in the USA
San Bernardino, CA
25 May 2014